BORDERLINE MOTHER

Unmask the negative impact of having a BPD mother,
understand the truth and the methods of healing the unique
wounds inflicted from infancy to adulthood

David Lawson PhD

TABLE OF CONTENTS

INTRODUCTION

Fear; that stupid feeling you can feel in your bones that makes you feel helpless and afraid, that sense that is telling you to back off, to give up. Anger; yet another thing you can't control and you feel is getting the better of you. That anger is stopping you from opening yourself up to others, but you need them; you can't be by yourself because you feel alone and afraid. As you look into the world, you see the people and the relationships you want, but you are afraid and insecure. That kind of closeness is what you need – you can feel that deep inside your soul – but you do not know how to approach them. You feel damaged and uncertain. You find yourself in a loophole, an endless, vicious circle of emptiness and you don't know how you ended up here. You just feel that you need to get out. You are not alone, so don't be afraid.

If you think that this your fault, please believe it is not. You're just one of many people in the dark and desperate for light. The first thing you have to realize is that it's not your fault. You must not blame yourself. You are not guilty, but the fingers of destiny and the unfortunate set of circumstances that led you to see the world in the way you do, have caused you to feel guilty about everything. This book is here to support you, to be with you and to help you. Its purpose is to help you understand that you are not to blame for the scars on your soul. Its purpose is to show you the truth and the truth is simple. You're the victim of a toxic relationship. You can't keep friendships, you don't trust others and you don't think there are good days ahead. That's not true; you have to know that. This is the most important part of your healing process and a way to get back on track. You are only a victim of an unhealthy relationship caused by living with your mother who suffered from Borderline Personality Disorder. Your mother was neither guilty nor aware that you were suffering. She loved you and wanted the best for you, however, her condition is the main reason you cannot trust others now. Don't resent your mother. After all, it wasn't her fault that she had Borderline Personality Disorder. Deep down, she loved you and you need to know that. But unfortunately, because of her life and her condition, she was not able to show that love for you and that is why today you feel that you are different from others.

You can't trust others, you can't build a stable relationship, you just can't open up to anyone because you're afraid you're never going to be able to trust those who enter your life. It's a very heavy burden to carry. You probably spent your entire life, or at least a good part of your childhood, in the prison your mind built in response to your mother's actions. You never knew what kind of day was waiting for you. You constantly felt loved and unwanted at the same time. At first, you thought it was all your fault or that such a relationship between you and your mother was normal. It made you feel weird seeing other kids having no such problems with their parents. You probably didn't understand why every day in that toxic relationship was different. One day you were the best thing in the world for her, the next, you were the worst and guilty of many things. You were often criticized and were unable to understand why all of this was happening. This book will help you learn that the world is different from the one you know. That you don't have to be withdrawn, or an outcast, and that you are not unwanted. Your value is not less than other people's, you are no less important than others. This book will help you understand that there is a whole other world out there, and that you can build a normal and stable connection with people. That you can love and that you will be loved.

What you went through and what you experienced was very difficult. The pain of living with a mother who suffered from Borderline Personality Disorder is a topic that has not been sufficiently researched and which is controversial because some do not consider Borderline Personality Disorder a disease.

Someone wise once said, "all happy families are the same, but every unhappy family is different and unhappy in its way." What is most important about all this is the fact that you are not alone. There are millions of other people who are just like you. And they all feel like you; lost, unable to carry the burden they have been struggling with since the very beginning of life. And they also feel trapped, hopeless and they think there they are worthless and unworthy of other people's love and attention. That is simply not true.

All the children who went through such a childhood were in constant pain and suffering because they thought they caused everything that happened to them, including the humiliation, and the verbal and physical violence, but they were only victims, nothing more. Many of them – perhaps including you – may have wondered if life is worth living. Many developed suicidal thoughts because they were confused and frightened from the very beginning of their lives. The sad truth is that all the children who grew up with mothers who suffered from this condition are only victims. Not all stories end well, but for you, just by being here today, reading this, means that your story is not over yet. This means that you have succeeded in spite of everything you went through. You should be proud of yourself. Life is worth living, remember that. This book will help you open your eyes, to understand that this is a great pain, but that you can overcome it. You can have friends, normal social relationships, a normal life.

Until now, you've been living on the edge, constantly wondering "how and why." Although Borderline Personality Disorder has ceased to be a social taboo and is now receiving increasing attention, we believe you did not know all about this severe mental condition. Borderline Personality Disorder is na very controversial term. Not only are there many disagreements between scientists and researchers about how this disorder occurs and how it develops. There is even an idea that the disorder does not exist at all. Some classification systems do not classify it as a disorder; others find that people with borderline pathology are increasingly encountering it. In the sea of different definitions, it is very difficult to find the answer to the question of what is or is not a Borderline Personality Disorder. In this book we will explain why this is not just your problem, every child in the same situation goes through the same thing. The logical question, then, is why is this the case?

The child is quite dependent on the mother in those early days and needs his mother's support and love for normal development. If he does not get what he needs, he will not be able to adequately resolve the separation and independence phase. As a result, the child will not develop into a mature personality, but will always use some of the primitive defense mechanisms, will not perceive other people as whole (because he or she will not be developmentally rounded), and will slip between the idealization and the impairment of other important persons from his or her environment. In the borderline state, we always encounter the following triad – aggression, depression and a vague identity. An inner void can have at least two meanings, which are by no means contradictory. It can refer to the physical and the psychic. In the first sense, a person can be empty when, for example, they are hungry. In the second sense, emptiness refers to effect, feeling, or absence of feeling. Emptiness, in the psychic sense, is a term that confuses many. For those who feel it and the experts who deal with it, the very word "emptiness" indicates the absence of something. Since it is a shortcoming, it is difficult to give a precise definition of what exactly is missing. Some authors talk about "feeling empty." However, that phrase is contradictory. Feeling indicates bias, polarization and, to put it bluntly, something. The void indicates "nothing." How can anyone feel nothing? If he feels something, is it the same as not feeling anything? That all seems very confusing and it is.

It turns out that the answer to this question is both difficult and paradoxical. When one is not feeling, that person has not developed any emotions about anything. When, however, one feels nothingness, that inner "nothing" is very intense and quite polarized and represents "something." To feel nothingness is to feel a significant unexplained amount of something we have no say in, something dead in us, something that has died and left its bad aspects in our interior, or something that never even came to life to make us feel alive inside.

Although statistics show that there are more borderline organizations than ever, the question is how many diagnoses have been properly established. Does this question necessarily arise if one has in mind the many disagreements of scientists about "what is this entity if we can call it an entity at all?" The sources of suffering for borderline individuals are unrecognized to them. A feeling of emptiness that leads to forced action – "acting out" is a term that represents the repetition of unconscious childhood patterns to overcome them in the present. As these childhood problems are unconscious, acting out cannot be resolved. Being around people brings a kind of immediate relief from tension, and on the other side, BPD persons might see this interaction as unbearable.

While there are many disagreements about borderline issues, it would be good to try to systematize some of the backbones that most agree with and to provide some kind of picture of borderline issues.

The main problems are the instability of self-understanding, interpersonal relationships, and mood swings. A characteristic pattern is a behavior characterized by instability of interpersonal relationships, self-experience, emotions, and control of emotions, which can be identified as a pattern in early adulthood. The condition is marked by great effort in avoiding real or fictional relationships, bonding with others and engaging in close relationships. Interpersonal relationships are volatile and intense. The identity of oneself is impermanent and disturbed. Impulsiveness is present in at least two of the following activities, which are potentially harmful to that person: negligent, promiscuous and excessive sexual behavior, drug abuse, excessive eating or drinking or spending money. Suicidal tendencies or suicide attempts may be present. Instead of suicidal thoughts, the borderline person can self-punish himself in various other ways (varieties of psychophysical self-harm). There is a chronic sense of emptiness. The feeling of anger is intense, difficult or impossible to control and (given the previously described acting out) is unsuitable for a particular situation.

According to official statistics, this type of disorder is present in about 1-2% of the population. The diagnosis is twice as common in females as in men. It's about emotionally immature, unstable, capricious and quarrelsome black and white worldviews. Such persons often have a misconception of themselves and other people, and they are unpredictable and unable to control their overwhelming (often destructive) emotions. In the event of a failure in their essential activities (work, college, emotional relationships, socializing) they often tend to engage in self-destructive behavior. This disorder is quite common in combination with other psychiatric disorders.

Borderline organized personalities are difficult, both to themselves and their environment. An inability to control emotions; a black and white worldview and impulsive reactions lead to both destructive and self-destructive behaviors. Although borderline people are not necessarily "giving up" people, relationships made with them are chaotic, intense, often short-lived, and usually very turbulent. They try to enter into relationships with others to regulate their tension and that can often fill others with a sense of emptiness. Borderline people can be in a state of idealism and euphoria, and others may think for a moment that they have succeeded in finding an ideal partner. But soon they can feel severe disappointment because the other person cannot patch up the gaping emptiness and chronic unfulfillment. Then there is the devaluation of the other person and, often, the search for someone new, the "ideal other," who unfortunately they will not be able to find. For every child, this is a terrible condition to grow up in. But you must understand, this is a very difficult social problem, mainly because the relationship between you and your mother is supposed to be the purest possible relationship. And this is not some kind of easily recognized condition. A BPD person lacks insight and the ability to see reality as it is. As such, he needs the help of another compassionate being to overcome difficulties and strike a balance in the chaotic world. Mother loves you and that is the main problem; no one who is looking can know for sure what is going on and you are trapped in the web of mixed emotions. That is why you feel like you are beneath everyone and that kind of feeling is quite normal; you simultaneously resent your mother but you love her too. We know that your self-confidence is shaken, but you can and will get better.

Your mother's condition is a very difficult mental state. This issue is so complex that many psychiatrists are unable to make the right diagnosis. Although this condition was first mentioned centuries ago, it was not given much importance. It is a great triad that develops in a person that can destroy a child. Your mother is an important part of your life; there is no doubt about it. This is why this is a very important topic. Everything begins with the mother. Each child looks for a warm hug, a nice word, a kiss, and tenderness. Showing tenderness and closeness to the child also helps these children understand what love is and to convey that love to their children when they become parents. This also applies to all other aspects of life, such as romantic relationships, partnerships of all kinds, and friendships. This is the primary reason you are unable to connect with people. In Borderline Personality Disorder, the mother is both addictive and aggressive and often has no boundaries. In moments she cannot see the difference between good and bad and you are the victim. To one who is only a child, anger and love are often torn out at the same time. You likely never understood it as a kid. We believe that one of the main problems for a child growing up in such a relationship is that the child cannot understand what is going on around him. The child has just arrived in the world, and is getting to know the world as he grows up. We think that the main problem is that the child cannot understand and compare.

This is precisely why the child gets a distorted picture of the world. We will give a banal example of the ability to understand and compare. We believe that the ability to compare is the ability to differentiate between different things. For example, someone may say that one cup is good or that it is bad because he has seen other cups. As he watched the cups, he developed the ability to figure out which cup is good and which is bad. It's the same with a child. But as a child, metaphorically speaking, you couldn't see other cups and that's the main problem. Your cup was your mother. You didn't have another mother. So you couldn't understand anything. For this reason, you and many other victims have developed a feeling that you are not worthy, that you are weak, that others are better.

You had to endure verbal and psychological violence. And you didn't know what was going on. You later learned to love your mother no matter what. Because after all, she's your mother who knew how to show you love from time to time. But you can help yourself, and you will. This book will help you to understand your problem, to confess to yourself that you have a problem and help you not to be judgmental to yourself. You can even help your mother. Although therapies can often be very long and difficult, research agrees that therapeutic assistance is beneficial for most borderline persons. Many therapies, however, are incomplete, and a "full recovery" does not always occur. However, by caring for and understanding the therapeutic relationship, borderline individuals often move towards a better, more integrated and fuller life. Just remember, you are here still, and by reading this book you are making a decision to heal your traumatic experience and to move on. That is priceless, and that is why you are a natural-born fighter and you will win in this fight also.

CHAPTER ONE: UNDERSTANDING THE BORDERLINE MOTHER

How do you understand someone who does not understand himself? Understanding a mother suffering from Borderline Personality Disorder is not easy. These are people who in many cases are unaware of their problem. They are high-risk, always conflict-ready, and difficult to reach. The usage of the term Borderline Personality Disorder (BPD) started in the 1930s, and the name was symbolically coined by Adolf Stern as the disorder is on the border between psychosis and neurosis.

Towards the end of the seventeenth century, English physician Thomas Sydenham wrote a frequently quoted sentence about a number of his patients in a letter: "They love the same ones beyond measure but they also hate them for no reason." He described their sudden outbursts of anger, pain, and fear. Of course, the disorder that Sydenham described was not called Borderline Personality Disorder (he choose the term "hysterical" for women and "hypochondriac" for men), but his description was a good prediction. Even today, the symptoms he cited are the two most important symptoms when making a diagnosis of Borderline Personality Disorder.

So this condition is not new. Symptoms have been reported earlier, but only in the last few decades have they become more significant. The severity of this condition is so big that it requires deep analysis.

The borderline condition is characterized by unsuccessful separation from the mother, which developmentally would normally occur at an early period. This failure to separate often comes because the mother (probably due to her problems) did not respond positively to the child's attempts to become independent, and to experiment with the world. The mother tends to be dismissive, depressed, or even angry when the child begins (naturally and developmentally normal) to separate from her and tries to get to know his wider environment.

We can say that early traumatic experiences and genetics are major factors in the development of Borderline Personality Disorder. All those suffering from this condition say they feel a void. It's a void they can't even describe to themselves. The main problem is that they are trying to bridge that gap through aggression, possessiveness or self-destruction. This is a very big problem, and it is of great importance when people suffering from this condition are mothers. The main problems are the instability of self-understanding, interpersonal relationships, and mood swings. A characteristic pattern is a behavior characterized by instability of interpersonal relationships, self-experience, emotions, and control of emotions, which can be identified as a pattern in early adulthood.

If the mother cannot understand herself, how can she understand the child? A mother with this condition is in a terrible position; she is both an aggressor and a victim. She is considered an aggressor because this condition leads to terrible behavior and a lack of empathy towards the child. Then, because of her condition, she terrorizes all the people around her and the child is best suited to serve as a pressure valve. On the other hand, the mother is also a victim because when the aggression, panic or other behaviors pass, she suffers, because she knows she has hurt the child. She suffers deeply and sincerely because she is aware that in the onset of anger, she hurt the innocent child she loves. Then in every way, she tries to make up for that outburst towards the child, so she acts protectively and she is then full of love for the child.

This lasts until the next attack caused by the condition, so the terrible cycle repeats. This leaves the child very confused and sad because he does not know or understand how the mother who loves him now hates him again. Of course, in this sad story, the child is the biggest victim, but we have to be objective; in most cases, the victim is also the mother who suffers because she hurts the child and cannot control herself.

Although this condition is followed by unstable emotions, and a tendency to experiencing strong euphoria and intense disappointment, borderline individuals are, in fact, mostly dysthymic. Dysthymia is a chronic, non-psychotic depressive disorder that lasts for at least two years and is characterized by a depressed mood and overall loss of life satisfaction. Therapies for people with these problems are, for the most part, long and difficult. The basic things that a therapist should offer to a borderline person are empathy (compassion), acceptance, as well as showing that he or she will be there and will stay with the client, will not leave him or impair him, and will be able to tolerate his sudden mood swings, anger, and often hatred and other self-destructive manifestations. Therefore, both the therapist and the client must "endure" the therapy. The shift is slow, but if a person is determined to accept help, they will, step by step, build up broken parts of their personality and reorganize early traumatic experiences. Borderline Personality Disorder is consistently inconsistent and stable in its instability. A BPD person lacks insight and the ability to see reality as it is. As such, he needs the help of another compassionate being to overcome difficulties and strike a balance in the chaotic world.

It is important to recognize this problem and help your mother, because the consequences are dreadful unless both mother and child are helped in time. One of the basic characteristics of Borderline Personality Disorder is emotional deregulation. Mothers with this disorder experience major mood swings accompanied by intense and sudden anger, often directed at their loved ones. In some cases, they have a personality that is "high risk" for conflict. This means that they have recurring patterns of behavior, where they focus their anger on specific offenders, which prolongs or escalates conflicts. If a child is a target, he needs to understand what this is all about. This is a major mental health problem that affects the relationships of millions of people every day. The main problem regarding Borderline Personality Disorder is related to living with a person who suffers from the disorder, especially when that someone is a person you depend on; your mother.

Causes of personality disorders are almost always associated with genetic predispositions when combined with the environment during childhood. The biopsychosocial approach to discovering the causes of personality disorders, i.e. the correlation of an individual's genetic, social and psychological background, is increasingly emphasized. Early childhood experiences have been shown to play almost the most important role in the development of the disorder. Excessive criticism, lack of attention, neglect, physical or psychological abuse, and many other childhood circumstances can be the trigger for a personality disorder that is already present in a person's genetic background. Often, different combinations of personality disorders also occur, so borderline personality disorder often occurs in combination with affective bipolar disorder.

The situation with the most consequences when it comes to Borderline Personality Disorder is certainly when the mother suffers from this disorder. This condition has devastating consequences on the children and if it's not properly recognized and treated it will most likely develop into the same condition in the child, or it will ruin the child's self-confidence for life.

Continuous entanglement in chaotic interpersonal relationships is one of the most recognizable features of Borderline Personality Disorder. In chronic avoidance of loneliness, these individuals often engage in dysfunctional relationships, despite intense feelings of victimization from partners.

So we know what it is like to live a life with the mother who suffers from this condition. She is constantly on edge; she loves and hates her child at the same time. If the relationship between mother and child occurs in the classic "nuclear" family, the child will often be forced to watch the constant verbal (and sometimes not just verbal) argument with the father. The child will often feel helpless and afraid in early childhood, but in the later years this will encourage rebellion within the child or the child will become lonely and associative, unable to trust anyone, and if the things escalate, that child will develop ideas that life is worthless and the idea of taking his own life and intensive thinking about suicide will occur. Yes, the pain is enormous and pressure is great, but you must understand that this is not your fault. You must see the problem with open eyes and be able to see the wider picture. Your mother may have scared you for life but do you still love her? Probably you do because you must understand that she did not ask for this, no one wants to be mentally ill. But the damage is done already, and you must go on.

The same thing will happen if the child is raised by a single mother who suffers from this condition, with the difference that mother may have numerous sexual partners and that can cause a whole new wave of traumas.

A mother is the beginning of everything. Even if she psychologically harmed her child, it is only a consequence of her poor childhood or poor relationship with her parents. A mother who often leaves her child with relatives, takes it too early to kindergarten, or needs more space for herself, her career or hobby can have a negative influence on the child. In adulthood, that child will have difficult relationships with the opposite sex: first, they will love to madness, then they will hate fiercely. In such cases, it is impossible to build a healthy relationship. In families where the child has been a judge in a quarrel between mother and father, later he will feel disrespect for himself, and for him, the lives of others will become more important than his own.

Children of single mothers often struggle to build their family because of feelings of guilt relating to their parents. Girls often have inappropriate relationships with men, and young men who are sensitive to women's suffering choose a woman who pities them and then suffer a lifetime of lack of love. If the mother cares for the child both physically and emotionally, the child will surely grow into a healthy person. Otherwise, they will not respect themselves; they will always place themselves in second or third place. The influence of the mother on the mental development of the child is one of the most significant and perhaps the most exploited topics in psychology. But this should not be surprising, given the fact that the quality of that emotional connection depends on what kind of relationship the child will have with himself and the people around him.

Children recognize and experience this connection with their mother primarily through the emotions they have about her. For example, a child who falls and scratches his knee generally runs toward his mother, knowing that she will help him feel better. This is because the mother is the primary source of security, and the father is a "knight in shining armor" who fights for the family and protects it. However, if we look at the mother with a personality disorder, we can almost certainly state that she had a traumatic childhood. Personality disorders originate from unstable family environments, with frequent losses and multiple parental substitutions in which deep and lasting relationships were not possible. Many of them were born as unwanted children and were never fully accepted. Others had parents who were ambivalent and hostile, who were lied to, physically beaten, or sexually abused. The role of trauma suffered in early childhood, as noted by some authors, is considered to be a key factor in the development of Borderline Personality Disorder in future mothers.

1.1. So what is so particular in understanding the mother with a borderline personality disorder? We have to analyze two questions. First; what is the role of the mother in the family and the child's life? And second; what is the core of Borderline Personality Disorder?

The role of a mother is crucial for the child. Many childhood scholars, especially those with psychoanalytic orientations, emphasize the importance of the mother in the development and upbringing of the child. First, there is an unbreakable biological bond between mother and child that grows into a deep emotional relationship. So that is the main problem for you; the biological bond is created by nature and you are unable to resist that bond. The love of a mother is a special kind of love. When someone rejects you, it can have severe consequences but we hope that you will learn how to cope with them and help yourself and your mother. Studies have shown that various anxiety states of the child, which can manifest even into adulthood, have a prenatal origin. More specifically, they are associated with the secretion of the maternal stress hormone, cortisol.

One aspect of the protective function of the mother is physical, that is, the child must be bathed, nourished, fed. Another form of protection is psychological, which is reflected in the child's safety when they are together. This form of protection is of great importance for the mental health of the child, as it is precisely the first emotions that are exchanged with the mother. Breastfeeding is not only about satisfying the urge to eat, but also about creating effective attachment. Attachment, as author and researcher Bolbi calls it, even influences the child's future partnerships. The baby cries, his mother takes the baby in her arms, gently rocking him and saying, "I'll kiss it better." The baby calms down from his mom's kiss and smiles. We know this situation; every mother has experienced it several times. A close relationship with the mother is the main driving force behind the baby's development in the womb and during the first six months after birth. Scientific research has confirmed that the unborn baby responds to the mother's mood and emotions. When the mother is upset, her fetus is upset as well. When the mother experiences short-term shock, the fetus remains cramped and disturbed for hours afterward. During all nine months of pregnancy, the baby is in inseparable physical and physiological contact with the mother. This cannot change abruptly after birth. When the baby comes into the world, she is not yet in the environment, but she perceives light, hears voices and feels pleasure from her mother's touch. That is why the physical closeness of skin to skin in the first hours after birth is so important. It remains important for many months to come. A mother's love is a fundamental physiological need that ensures development, as is food.

Regarding the other question, the answer is very difficult. Arrieti calls borderline personalities "tornado personalities." She says that they often live in an atmosphere of "disaster and doom," chronically dissatisfied, disappointed, with a constant sense of deprivation, but at the same time they show resilience, a sense of humor and "phoenix phenomena" (persistently "getting up" after frequent "falls"). They complain about alienation from people, they are desperate for the meaninglessness of living, it is easy to recognize them by the leitmotif of their verbalization; "There is a great inner void in me."

You cannot look at a mother with this condition only as the offender. She is a victim too, because she is not incapable of loving. On the contrary, she suffers. She suffers terribly and later she tries to repair everything with the child. So you may have experienced another trauma. Mothers bond with children and there is no exception. She may later try to keep the child, to not let him grow up because she wants him to be with her forever.

Only the aggressive type of mother will cause the child to develop anger. But you need to know that these cases are common and you are not alone. This consequence has affected many people and in this story, they are all victims. If you are a survivor of this trauma, be strong, encourage yourself to seek professional help and overcome the problems that have arisen because you will realize that you are no less important than others. Your worldview will open up, but you must know that nothing was your fault, and it was not your mother's. If you understand and forgive, you have already taken the first step towards healing. Only great people are forgiving and you must be aware that no one wanted this to happen. Not you, of course, and not your mother.

CHAPTER TWO: HOW IT HAD TO BE

If you remain in the stage of remembrance and keep looking over your shoulder, you will grow old alone looking into the past. It's not a good place, it's called the past for a reason. What you need to know first and foremost is that the past must be left behind. As long as you look out the window of the past, you will remain there forever. If you look and wonder what could have been different, you will miss a lot. First of all, you will miss the future. Worst of all, you won't be aware of the present. Many opportunities will pass, trains will come and pass and you won't see them. You will look back. That's why we tell you to stop looking at yesterday. Remember – yesterday ceased to exist today.

It was not easy in the family you grew up in. It is hard for you, we understand. Your main problem is that you wake up every day with the same question popping into your head. And you're not the only one. Many others who have survived a mother with Borderline Personality Disorder may be having the same or similar thoughts. When you open your eyes after a bad night's sleep – because we know that every night is a challenge for you – you ask yourself, "Why me? Why are others happy and I'm miserable?" and so on. That little voice becomes your constant companion. When you lie down to rest, the voice does not allow you to relax and calm down because it reminds you that your childhood left a wound on your soul that will be waiting for you in the morning. That little voice doesn't go away. It will be there every morning. You have to wake up from reality, you have to wander off from yourself, you have to stop the issues that bring you back to the past. Because that reality that is like a nightmare – with the difference that you know everything is real and that there is no escape; you have to wake up. This book is here to help you understand who you are, to understand that life can and should be better.

We know you've never been like other kids. Your role in the family was to be a metaphorical punching bag. You served as a bucket for emptying someone else's emotions into. Your mother hit you with her unstable emotions because of her disorder. She emptied her frustration through you. You looked at your friends who were simply children. Your friends enjoyed their childhood, being loved constantly while you were caught in a swirl of emotions. In the holidays, your Christmas tree was probably beautiful one day and destroyed the next. Being a sponge to your mother and absorbing all her bad feelings was, unfortunately, your role.

You deserve to be loved as a kid. You were loved but you were also constantly the best person for your mother to unload her frustration on. Your father either objected, and you witnessed terrible quarrels and physical altercations between your father and mother as your father tried to share that burden with you. Maybe you had a father who decided to stay away and to not interfere. Maybe you resent him for that. There was no one to defend you. While you were trying to understand the world, no one understood you. It's a terrible pain. You felt betrayed, especially when you compared yourself to other children and listened to stories of happy families. But your family was different. You kept repeating the same pattern that you eventually adopted because you didn't know you that you needed something different. In a way, you laid your head before destiny and reconciled with it. You knew every new day was a challenge and you didn't know what was waiting for you. You used to be able to watch TV and play and sometimes you had to sit while crying in the dark wondering why. It's a question you still haven't resolved today. It's a question you have to clear if you want to get ahead and beat this. We are sure you want to help yourself because you are reading this book. That's why we're sure you'll make it. We'll look at what your family was supposed to be like. What did you miss in your childhood?

2.1. What does a healthy family look like?

Family is an irreplaceable environment in which a person forms himself as a person, in which he lives and satisfies some of his most important needs. The family is such a social community that every individual feels the need for because it is the foundation of the whole of human life. That is why it is of vital importance for every member of the social community.

During childhood, the child needs to be given as much love as possible, since this later reflects on his life in adulthood, his interaction with the environment, and affects his openness to others, and love and understanding for another. By satisfying the child's need for love and tenderness, a sense of security, safety, acceptance and belonging in society develops. From these feelings, a sense of self develops. Parents' behavior serves as a model for children to strive to identify with. Therefore, mutual respect, mutual assistance, and love between spouses and parents and children, which is characteristic of most modern families, is an important encouraging example for a young being. Of several factors that influence the development of a child and the formation of a person's personality, the family is one of the most important.

Family and family education represent the first and fundamental stage in the development of a child and his or her personality, and they cannot be replaced by anything. The family differs from other social groups by the social role it plays in the life of each individual, in that it provides a much more concrete impetus for the development of man as a human being. It also differs in the functions it performs, which are not primarily aimed at society, but also individual members. The individual today feels the need for the family as a community. In all societies so far, the family in its most generalized context is formed based on the specific social institution of marriage, which indicates that the family is a socially regulated community of opposite sexes within the allowed form.

In a family where each parent plays their part, the emphasis is placed on the children and the children themselves learn through that love to return the same love later to their children.

If we want to understand the importance of the modern family in personality development, we will explain its most frequently mentioned functions and especially the educational function, as well as some of its characteristics and development throughout history. The family is a specific bio-social community of people. It plays a very significant role in the development not only of man, but of society in general. Family is a mediator between society and the individual, but the family performs more functions than any other social group. By forming a family, a person is perceived as a social being in such a way that his life has a completely different sense of purpose compared to when he had no spouse or children.

All household members under one roof are family. It is also a group of people with common ancestors, common descent. The word "family" today refers to different terms. In the broadest sense, it is an inseparable whole of persons connected by marriage or adoption or the birth of an individual who inherits lineage, gender, and dynasty. In the narrower sense, the word "family" means relatives living under the same roof – or even simply a father, mother and children.

That feeling of warmth is irreplaceable. It brings a sense of security in which you know that someone will always protect you, no matter what. You know you can share your problems and you know that someone will stand up for you and show you the right way. Family makes us who we are. We gain our worldviews through our family values. We learn from our parents. Although there are exceptions, numerous studies have shown that many children will imitate their parents. Children want to repeat their parents' patterns of behavior. That is why when children witness violence in their family, they see it as normal behavior.

But through this book, you're hopefully already beginning to realize that this doesn't have to be you. Just because you witnessed violence as a child, you don't necessarily have to be a bully to your children and loved ones. You need to understand that all this is very bad. Some children have been in bad families and grow into great parents who never show violence because they realized that it was bad, and that just because they went through it, their children don't have to. Your kids don't have to be victims. There are many examples of bright and caring parents who were strong enough to not let their childhood fears and the traumas they endured affect their children.

Every family goes through different stages. The family encompasses two types of interrelated but distinct relationships in which biological, psychological and social elements intersect: satisfying the sexual urges and emotional needs of people, giving birth to and raising children. Although these categories may also take place outside the family, they mostly occur within the family.

2.2. Home family

A family begins when two people decide to live together. This stage is characterized by teaching partners to be a dyad/twosome, which involves setting internal organization and boundaries. The difficulty of this phase is that it is not just two individuals, but two products of their family backgrounds that nurture different cultural values and have different expectations. In partnership at this stage, it is important to be flexible so as to reach a consensus on issues of money, religion, recreation, friends, household chores, and shared free time. The problems specific to this phase of family development are the establishment of rules and conflicts that accompany this process, the distribution of responsibilities, lack of respect for diversity, and difficulties forming family boundaries.

2.3. A family with a very young child

The second stage involves the pregnancy and birth of the first child when the parental roles are established, which involves the distribution of care, authority and power, and participation in the upbringing process. This life stage is also characterized by the development of patterns of emotional attachment of a child to the mother in the first years of the child's life. This is different from the first months of life during which the child is dependent on the mother in terms of satisfying physiological needs. The problems that arise during this period are conflicts of responsibility, unwillingness to play a parental role, and a pushing of the external boundaries of the family system.

2.4. A family with a preschooler

This developmental phase begins after the couple's adaptation to the formed triad. This phase is characterized by specific tasks concerning the psychosexual development of the child and adapting the child's upbringing to his age. This process should take place in the protective and safe atmosphere that parents provide for the child. At this stage, the child goes through significant stages of psychosexual development, and parents exert an influence on his or her need for tenderness, rejection, defiance, and affection, etc. At this stage, parents introduce the child into the world of interpersonal relationships, shaping his personality, educating him and being a model for the child.

2.5. A family with a school-aged child

In this life cycle, the child begins the process of socialization, acquires working habits and learns responsibilities. Differences in parental involvement may cause difficulties in the child's adaptation to the new circumstances. At this stage, the relationship to external systems and the permeability of family boundaries are examined, on which the external impact of the school and the wider social environment will affect the family. The most common problems of the family in this life stage are problems related to the learning and behavior of the child, school phobia, etc. In the background of these problems are the most common unresolved parental or marital conflicts.

2.6. A family with an adolescent

The time of adolescence of the eldest child is characterized by the adolescent's need for a greater degree of independence and acceptance of new values outside the family while testing the limits of parental authority. The rebellion against parents by which adolescents develop their own identities can become a problem, which may be a continuation of earlier emotional and developmental difficulties that have not been adequately addressed. This period is also characterized by a re-, view of the permeability of borders. If the boundaries are too closed and the family does not allow external influences to penetrate, family relationships are networked and the rules become rigid. Such family dynamics do not provide an opportunity for adequate development and the differentiation of young people. If the family boundaries are too open to allow uncritical penetration of outside influence, the family runs the risk of losing its identity. If the family cannot change, it faces the problem of adolescent-parent conflict.

2.7. The departure of children from their parents

The time of separation of children from their parents may be considered the most stressful event in the life span of a family. Children need to leave, and parents rethink their roles, often unwilling to adapt to new circumstances. Parents try to keep their children in the family environment, unaware of the serious difficulties their endeavors can bring. Therefore, the family, in contrast to its function, becomes a risk factor, not a child and youth protection factor. At this stage, the family most often faces the problems of delayed separation of young people from their parents, insecurity, and fear of independence.

2.8. The postpartum family

This phase of family development is characterized by an "empty nest" in which the partners are alone again without children in their homes. After many years during which the primary preoccupation was the upbringing of children, partners face the need to re-adjust to new life situations, change the way they communicate, and regulate closeness and distance in the relationship.

2.9. An old family

This phase is characterized by aging parents, which leads to a change in self-image, the challenge of coping with health issues, and loss of one or both partners. Age contributes to social exclusion and the also leads to the efforts of elderly parents to break the boundaries of their children's family system, which can most often be recognized in their attempts to engage in the care of grandchildren. Each stage of family development has its specificities. The time of transition from one life stage to another is a source of internal stress as the transition requires a change in the way the family functions. At each transition point from one life stage to another, the functionality of family relationships from the previous period is reviewed. Going through the trajectory of one's development, the family goes through developmental stages to adapt to the requirements of the life cycle in which it is located.

These processes, shaped by the beliefs and value system of previous generations, customs, secrets, and myths, create a family culture that defines all-important issues of one family, including how to emotionally bond and separate members.

But in a dysfunctional family like yours, problems have been created that are now yours.

2.10. A functional family

The term "functional" refers to something capable of fulfilling its purpose or function. However, it is not possible to reach a definitive definition of a functional family by a pure analogy, since the assessment of whether a family is functional or dysfunctional depends on the goals the family sets for itself, the value system, the life cycle and the satisfaction of economic and cultural needs. Just as the modern family questions the comprehensive definitions of the family for a variety of reasons, so can a "functional," "normal" or "healthy" family be viewed as a social construction determined by continuous change in a world that is also constantly changing.

Also, our personal experience, language, and professional orientation influence the perception of this term. You can see that the functionality of a family depends not only on the relationships that exist between family members but also on the relationship between family and society. The primary social task of the family is to ensure the socialization and humanization of man, that is, to create the development of those traits in the personality that will allow for good adaptability, but this should not necessarily mean a conformist attitude towards society. All authors who have dealt with family functionality point out that those functional families should have a solid parental alliance. Parents use authority based on maturity and fairness with understanding, respect, cooperation and a warm relationship.

A functional family, among other things, is largely determined by cohesion, a shared home, communication between family members and interactions between generations. Of course, a family in a formal sense can exist without all these determinants, but then it loses its psychological meaning. It is precisely the family of communities where there is a sense of belonging and solidarity. Each family will be all the more content and functional if there is a willingness on the part of those who join such a community to fulfill and mutually fulfill important human needs (closeness, trust, cooperation), and not only to achieve specific goals (reproduction, economic security or gaining social status).

A functional family has a flexible structural power with shared authority, clear family rules, unbroken generational boundaries and a style that fosters association. Family members have their individuality and ability to determine closeness and distance, can tolerate disagreements and uncertainty, communicate freely and spontaneously, and accept the diversity and sensitivity of others. Humor, tenderness, and care are integral to the family atmosphere. Conflict is openly discussed and problems are identified and resolved. Given the different understandings and definitions of the functional family within system theory and theoretical models of systemic family therapy, an overview of theoretical and clinical points of view can be summarized in four major concepts in defining family normality:

According to this concept, whose origins are in the medical model, a normal or healthy family is one in which there are no symptoms or disorders in any family member. The limitation of this approach lies in the fact that it is based on the absence of pathology (negative criteria) and ignores indicators of positive functioning. Healthy family functioning is more than the absence of symptoms or problems. Similarly, another limitation of this concept stems from the realization that there may be some simple correlation between family functioning and the health of the individual. It would be wrong to assume that every individual disorder is related to dysfunction in the family, as well as to assume that a healthy individual necessarily comes from a healthy family.

2.11. Normal family as average (normality as mediocrity)

In this concept, which has a foothold in the social sciences and is formed based on statistical indicators for presenting reality, the family is normal or healthy if it is typical and if it is in line with what is common and expected for ordinary families in a given context. A limitation of this approach is the ability to fall into the trap of equalizing optimal functioning of the family with severely dysfunctional ones, as they both deviate significantly from the normal distribution.

2.12. Normal family as optimal (normality as optimal)

This approach defines a normal family through optimal functioning with ideal features, which is a utopia. The limitation of this concept stems from the fact that the norms of an ideal family are socially and culturally constructed values that "prescribe" what families should be. However, patterns that are optimal for one family may not meet the standards of the ideal in a given environment, which does not mean that that family is not functional.

2.13. Normal family relationships (Normality as a process)

This approach, which rests on general system theory, defines the normality of the family through the normality of family processes. Unlike other approaches that look at normality statically, this approach does not think of a normal family as an immutable, timeless entity. Seeing normality as a process that varies depending on the internal needs of the family and the external needs of the wider systems constantly questions both continuity and change throughout the life cycles of the family. If we take into account the concepts of a systematic approach to the family that we have discussed in the previous section, then it can be said that functionality has the meaning of usability of the family pattern (the way the family functions) in achieving family goals. Therefore, normal family functioning is a process that takes place over time in a particular socio-cultural context, and through which, through developmental interactions, the basic tasks of the family are accomplished.

Such a functional family is characterized by the connection of members to a community characterized by a mutual relationship with trust, closeness, mutual care and support. There exists a balance between autonomy and reciprocity, and an environment in which there is an appreciation of individuality and intimacy, which has a respect for individual differences and autonomy. A functional family gives impetus to individual maturation care, socialization of children and cares for other vulnerable family members. There is organizational stability with clear roles and boundaries, adaptability, capacity for change, flexibility concerning internal and external demands, effective methods for coping with stress, open, clear and warm communication, effective and creative negotiation and the ability to use a wide range of behaviors and strategies in conflict resolution. The generally accepted belief system of a functional family enables trust and connection with past and future generations, and there exists adequate resources for basic economic security and psychosocial support through a network of extended family and friends, the community and wider social systems.

This definition of a functional family needs to be complemented by the trait of such a family that it can grow, despite any difficulties it encounters. A healthy family is always looking to expand their experiences. The difficulty is seen in such a family as a way for the family to increase its experience and growth. A healthy family, therefore, has the resources to solve their problems. Joy and humor are the strengths of a healthy family. Humor alleviates tension, allows for communication without confrontation, and adds emotional intensity to problematic situations.

2.14. A dysfunctional family

The term "dysfunctional" refers to something that works wrong or doesn't work at all. Unlike functionality, it is much easier to understand what the term dysfunctional is in one family system. If we started from the assumption that any change in the life cycle of a family brings stress, then a dysfunctional family would represent that family that is unable to adapt to the new living conditions and cannot cope with stress without major consequences. In such families, there are extremes in the connection of its members, so that the boundaries between the members are deleted or the members are very far apart. The borders to the "outside world" are also not permeable. The dysfunctional family is most often either isolated from the outside world without a formed family identity with inflexible and strict rules, or the boundaries are so open that anything that comes from the outside world is uncritically accepted.

The roles in dysfunctional families are not clearly defined, so often children assume parental roles. Communication is vague, confusing and contradictory, messages are not listened to or accepted and there is only minimal verbal exchange with frequent mystification. Such a family always delays problem-solving. The family is constantly in a state of crisis that is not recognized until one or more family members have a symptom or when the family threatens to break up.

2.15. Symptoms of dysfunctional families:

A dysfunctional family can be characterized by lack of empathy understanding, and sensibility towards individual family members, while on the other hand there is an expression of extreme empathy towards one or more family members who have a "special status." Other symptoms include denial (refusal to acknowledge the existence of undesirable conduct) inadequate or non-existent personal boundaries, disrespect for other people's borders extremes in conflict (or too much strife or insufficient discussion between family members), unequal and unfair relationship rules towards one or more family members due to their gender, age, ability, race, economic status, etc., and high levels of jealousy and other controlled behaviors. Dysfunctional families may also include divorced parents, parents in constant conflict or parents who should have separated but did not (at the expense of their child). Dysfunctional families lack time spent together, especially recreational activities and social events ("We never do anything as a family"). They may also be characterized by unacceptable sexual conduct (adultery, promiscuity or incest) and an environment in which children are afraid to talk about what is happening at home (inside or outside the family), or otherwise feel afraid of their parents and other family members. Family members may not acknowledge each other, and (or) refuse to be seen together in public (either unilaterally or bilaterally). It is also important to emphasize that dysfunctional patterns at one level (e.g. maintaining an unstable marriage) can also be dysfunctional at another level (in this case the subsystem of children).

If we include wider social systems in the assessment, we can also identify their dysfunctionality concerning the family (e.g. schools or kindergartens), so interventions sometimes need to be addressed not only to the family but also to wider systems that can be a source of dysfunction. When a family is faced with a crisis or becomes aware of the presence of symptoms or dysfunctional relationships, then it must be willing to change.

It is a common belief that the parents' love for the child is instinctive, biologically given and that it manifests itself at his birth. In reality, the birth of a child begins a process in which a long-lasting and stable emotional connection between the child and the person caring for him or her is gradually developed. This process of shaping emotional closeness, the most important part of which takes place in the first year of a child's life, is called the daily love of mother and child. In professional literature, this is the so-called "emotional attachment". Because the mother typically spends the most time with the child in that earliest relationship, we will hereafter refer to the mother, although the primary caregiver may also be the father, grandmother or someone else who is the closest to the child.

Early childhood is very important; we might say essential for the child. A strong emotional attachment and communication between the child and the mother develops most intensively in the first year. A child's need for such a relationship is of evolutionary origin and is part of a survival system. An infant who is unprotected and helpless in his or her immaturity is more likely to survive if protected by one person's proximity. Separation from this person causes intense fear in the child. The fear of separation first appears at the age of 6 to 8 months and is most pronounced by the 18th month.

Fear is also an indicator that the child has established this important emotional closeness with one person. A child needs to have a calm, stable and sensitive person with him/her who will be able to respond to his/her needs and provide him/her with security and love. If not, the infant and toddler will not develop well, not only emotionally, but also intellectually and physically. The mother-father relationship is extremely important, so too the father's feelings towards the child, which greatly influence the quality of the mother's role.

Experience shows that no pressures are good. If the mother is in circumstances that are difficult for her, she may have repulsive and aggressive feelings towards her child. This is a taboo topic. And it is in this situation that the mother needs the understanding, support and assistance of the family and a professional, a person to whom they will be able to express their feelings and thoughts without condemnation. Here, the crucial role of the father and the wider family is to support the mother-child relationship with patience and understanding. The love and security that a child experiences in their earliest childhood are an important prerequisite for the later development of a normal and healthy personality. In this earliest emotional relationship, basic personality traits are formed, which are difficult to change afterward. These experiences depend to a large extent on how much the child will be capable of love when he or she grows up and how they will experience themselves and the world around them (the so-called basic picture of the world); whether he thinks it is good and deserves the love of other people or is does not deserve it; is the world around him good and ready to help when needed? These first contacts with the environment largely depend on how much later, in childhood and adulthood, he will believe in himself and other people and be able to achieve in life what he wants and what makes him happy. The love and security gained in the early years is successful in prevention of later disorders: behavioral disorders, delinquency, addiction, violence and abuse, and other evils of the modern age that afflict parents. The development of brain structures and the way of raising children at an early age are physically connected.

Attachment issues arise when a mother does not respond to the need of a child who is seeking her. These mothers reject the child's need for attachment, dislike intimate, face-to-face contact, especially when the baby wants it. They can talk about their baby in warm words, be a play partner, be diligent about feeding and sleeping, but when a child shows a need for physical and emotional closeness, it becomes threatening for them (because they may have felt left out during childhood). Such children show little or no caution to strangers and only become upset when left alone. They show a lack of collaboration, exploratory behavior, and empathy, have poor relationships with peers, avoid close emotional attachments, feel that emotions are not important, resulting from a defensive self-protective adaptation to expecting rejection by the mother in stressful situations. Avoiding affectionate adults shows fear of intimacy, and lack of confidence in people. Such people may feel uncomfortable when close to others, and become nervous and repulsive if they get too close. Anxiety attachment arises as a result of the mother's behavior in which she sometimes responds to the child's need for closeness and is available and sometimes unavailable. As a result, these children perceive the mother (or other attachment figure) as inconsistent, at times supportive, at times unsupportive, causing them to become insecure and fearful, and perceive all adult figures as unreliable. As a consequence, children's confidence and self-esteem as well as motivation to explore the environment will depend on the support and approval of the mother. This dependence on others hinders the development of adequate emotional connections and leads to emotional instability and sensitivity to stress.

So with these examples and information, you are slowly getting the information you already know deep down. You now know all the major facts. But you must realize that just because you have missed a lot you mustn't look back in anger. Focus on tomorrow, focus on the future.

You were a victim in a family that did not fulfill its purpose. Instead of happiness, you got sadness and now you look at the past and that disturbs you. You must have asked yourself a thousand times

"What am I doing here?" Because of your lack of love, you began to doubt yourself; you began to disbelieve in better. Don't despair; you must never give up hope. Hope and will are your salvation. And the understanding you need you will gain by reading this book. You will understand what your recovery path is. There is a way; you must never give up on yourself. This book will give you guidelines for recovery and a better life.

You have to know one more thing; no one succeeds alone. We all need people around us who help us to see that path of recovery. You will find your way. You've already taken a step toward recovery with this book. Believe in yourself and let this book be a guide. In that way, that little voice in your head that accompanies you to bed every night and wakes you up every morning will start to fade and eventually it will completely disappear.

CHAPTER THREE: THE MAIN STYLES OF A BORDERLINE MOTHER

3.1. The unfortunate truth

Every disease is the same in one respect. Every illness, whether mental or physical, occurs in many variations. So it is in some ways useless to cut off a branch when the disease is at the very root of the tree. The disease is in the person. People are not afraid of illness, people are more afraid of the healing process. This is not due to fear of medicines, but because most people think they are relieved of their moral obligations due to illness. This condition is very specific. There is a fine line between a sense of morality and aggression in Borderline Personality Disorder. Thus, Borderline Personality Disorder is no different to other illnesses in the sense that it can occur in different forms. The most sensitive group are mothers because their role in society is essential. The mother is the one who instills moral values and makes a man from a child.

3.2. Specifics of BPD

Your pain is what makes you different, more specific, and your suffering is great because you grew up in such a situation. You have no one to complain to about it because you don't think anyone understands you. That's where you have made a mistake. You are afraid of disappointing others because you feel you are less valuable. All these feelings in you are caused because your mother suffered from Borderline Personality Disorder. You need to understand that your mother showed symptoms of her condition and that they were different depending on what variation of her condition appeared.

The pain you carry within yourself is the result of variations on the conditions your mother struggled with. So again, do not blame your mother; she did not choose to have this condition and she did not want you as her child to be injured in any way.

3.3. The main styles of a borderline mother

It can be concluded that there are several types of borderline mother, the main ones being:

1. Discouraged borderline

2. Impulsive borderline

3. Petulant borderline

4. Self-destructive borderline

3.4. Depression and anger

The first type of borderline mother is the so-called "discouraged borderline". That kind of mother is often very needy and dependent. The main paradox is that this type of borderline mother is particularly dangerous because even though they are needy and dependent and even insecure, they simultaneously harbor a lot of anger in them. They have a strong desire for acceptance and approval, but they are also very insecure and they have feelings of inferiority, so they are both depressed and they have a sudden outbursts of aggression. If they don't find proper approval, they will become marginalized and seriously depressed. That depression is not a joke. If they are not treated well it could evolve into suicidal thinking and possible tragedy.

In this case, you probably dealt with so many bad things. You probably had to go through a lot to please your mother because you were afraid of what would happen if you weren't with her.

3.5. Pure rage

An impulsive borderline mother tends to be very charismatic, energetic, and they are very good company. People love to be around them because their impulsive behavior can be very appealing to people. But the downside of this type is their need to be the center of attention. The mother with this type of Borderline Personality Disorder will be fun, but she is also "the drama queen." She will often heavily neglect the child's needs because she must be the center of attention. This type of mother will be abusive, self-centered, and she will act rashly and she will not care for possible consequences.

In this case, you suffered terrible consequences because you were a victim in every way. To deal with this type of mother is extremely difficult. But you endured, you're still here and that's the most important thing.

3.6. What went wrong?

The petulant borderline mother can't be pleased. She will always complain about everything because she is always right. She has a constant need to argue, to fight, to have an outbursts of anger, and that kind of behavior is a living nightmare. She will provoke conflict without any reason. She is stubborn and she doesn't know to say "I'm sorry." In that kind of relationship, the mother will set up a task and she will have an outburst of anger towards the child and that child will never get recognition for any effort. It will become a person with no self-respect because in this type of relationship the child will always be the "guilty party." Later in life, this will result in major consequences for the child. They will become a person who doesn't trust anyone, who doesn't appreciate himself and a big hole will appear regarding social relations and contact.

"You are not good, you know nothing, you are not worth it, you are wrong." If you heard a lot of these words during your childhood and grew up while trying to please your mother without success, no matter how good you were for everyone else, then you are the victim of this type of Borderline Personality Disorder your mother suffered.

3.7. Please don't do this

The self-destructive borderline mother is her own worst enemy. She tends to all kinds of dangerous behavior. She lacks a stable sense of self, she is also dependent and she has a constant fear of abandonment. This type of borderline mother will often try to get away from her inner problems by experimentation with various drugs, alcohol and other risky behaviors. She will always be bitter, moody, and filled with anger that she can't properly express. That is what leads to various types of arguing, and provoking others. The child will suffer a lot because it can't control this kind of behavior and that will lead to fights and abandonment. A consistent pattern of neglect and abuse will occur and it will result in loathing.

"I want to kill myself; my life doesn't mean anything... Mom, don't please, I love you" is a common phrase that characterizes this variation of Borderline Personality Disorder. You probably had to hide drugs, alcohol and other destructive substances because you feared your mother would abuse them.

3.8. Look up and never look back

Today you have to take a different attitude, no matter how much you have suffered through life. Many people like you are still struggling with this and trying to understand how and why. You have to stop this and tell yourself loudly, "The world changed me and because of that I suffered, today I want to change myself and because of that I am wise."

Life has shown you his teeth, you've survived terrible things, now it's time to fight back and take a stand.

It doesn't matter that they say, "It's easier to make a strong kid than to repair a broken man." No matter how broken you feel, you can be again yourself.

The scars you wear are a reminder how many times life tried to break you, but every single time you survived – because you are a warrior.

CHAPTER FOUR: TYPES OF ABUSE

It's not the point of this chapter to serve as a painful reminder of what you've been through. This chapter should serve as a guide for you to see what other types of abuse exist, besides the ones you survived. The purpose of this part of the book is not to make it difficult for you and make you experience bad memories, but to show you that you are not alone. That there are many others who have experienced what you have, and that abuse can take many forms.

Abuse is not only what you see with the naked eye; it can be much more complex than broken bones and bruises on the body. Although less noticeable, psychological violence against children leaves much more severe consequences, which often come to light several years after the abuse. It can permanently damage a child's mental health and have serious consequences for his or her personality and that is the case when it comes to abuse from a borderline mother.

Emotional abuse is the most insidious, and even the most dangerous, when it comes to a child's development. It gradually kills the child's feeling of being wanted and loved, their sense of their own identity, security, reality, and relationship with the world. The possibilities of neglect and abuse of children are very diverse in both ways and intensity. Emotional neglect and abuse are far more common in everyday life than physical and sexual ones.

Every day, the child is felt by various actions and words that he or she is guilty and responsible for all the inconveniences, failures and dissatisfactions of the parents, that at his/her birth he/she began to endanger the life of the family. A young child cannot grasp the illogicality and unreasonableness of these remarks and accusations – he or she begins to feel guilty and sometimes even encourages this abuse through his or her behavior.

When a mother does not intentionally show love to a child to punish him for his misconduct, it is a form of psychic violence. These actions are often accompanied by a verbal message such as "I no longer love you because you were naughty."

4.1. The six most common forms of child abuse by a borderline mother

Rejection involves a large group of heterogeneous behaviors that (intentionally or unknowingly) send a message that a child is unwanted, unloved, bad, wrong. Child abuse or neglect of a child's emotional needs is a common form of emotional abuse against children. Telling your child to get out, calling them derogatory names, making a child a "scapegoat or black sheep" in the family, and blaming them for family problems are common forms of rejection. Refusing to talk to or hold a child, and refraining from cuddling, touching, kissing and hugging has the same effect.

Constant criticism: ("You never try ... You don't do anything right ... How many times do you need to be told? ... What is your problem? ... Will you ever remember it? ... I worry what will happen to you ...") Examples of constant criticism include:

- Comparison of the child to peers at the expense of the child

- Telling the child it's ugly

- Yelling or swearing at the child

- Misrepresentation and use of labels such as "nerd," "idiot," "jerk," "fool," "whore," "incompetent," "slug," "drug addict."

- The constant humiliation of a child through a joke

- Constant teasing of a child for his physical appearance

- Regret that the child is not of the opposite sex

- Refusal to hug or express love physically ("Too tired, nervous, not comfortable, tired, doing something alone, boring, hard …")

Abandoning a child can include:

- Excluding a child from family activities,

- Treating an adolescent as a child

- Removing a child from the family (sending to relatives, boarding schools, camps…)

- Allowing a child to make decisions that are not appropriate for his or her age

- Refusing to spend time with a child or play with him

Ignoring is a form of rejection, but unlike rejection, there is no (conscious or unconscious) intention. Ignorance is common in adults whose emotional needs were not satisfied as children, and as a result, they are often completely insensitive to the needs of their children. Such parents are unable to connect with the child or provide adequate care. They sometimes fail to notice the child's presence at all. Many times such parents are only physically present. Failure to respond to the child's requests for connection or lack of interaction with the child psychological abuse. It can also include:

- Non-response to a child's spontaneous social behaviors (smiles, handshake, giggling, questions…)

- Not paying attention to significant events in the child's life (birthday, school events, New Year's, sports competitions ...)

- Refusing to talk about school activities, or the child's interests…

- Planning activities or vacations without children

- Failure to provide adequate health care to the child

- Non-involvement of the child in daily activities.

Intimidation: Borderline mothers use threats, shouting, and physical punishment to inflict serious psychological harm on their children. Separating a child to criticize and punish or ridiculing her for expressing emotion is abusive behavior. Threatening children with cruel words, beatings, abandonment or death is unacceptable. Witnessing domestic violence is also one of the worst forms of abuse of a child; the child does not have to be directly exposed or be the physical victim of that violence for damage to occur.

Child isolation: A parent who uses isolation as a form of child abuse may not include the child in age-appropriate activities, may keep the child isolated in their room without adequate stimulation necessary for the child's development, or may prevent a teen from socializing and having extracurricular activities. Requiring a child to spend time exclusively in his or her room, denying meals with his family, or separation from the rest of the family and peers can be destructive to the child. Some parents may allow their child to use drugs and alcohol, witness the cruel treatment of humans and animals, watch inappropriate sexual content, witness or be guilty of criminal activities (theft, assault, prostitution, gambling). Encouraging a minor child to engage in activities that are illegal or potentially dangerous is child abuse.

It doesn't matter that the definitions of violence against children are numerous, they all inflict pain, physical or psychological damage, endanger the health and physical or mental integrity of the individual and impede the normal development of a minor.

The most common and visible form of violence against children is physical violence. It comes in many forms, most commonly: hitting, slapping, burning, throwing on the floor or downstairs, tying to a radiator or closet, denying food, locking in an attic or basement, administering toxic substances, alcohol or inappropriate medications, biting, attempts to drown or choke a child, etc. Physical abuse is most often accompanied by emotional abuse and neglect. There are numerous consequences of such abuse.

Mental abuse or emotional deprivation is a relationship or behavior that neglects, threatens, underestimates, offends or verbally attacks a minor's personality and displays negative feelings about them. The forms of emotional deprivation include the denial of parental love and emotional support, rejection in the form of indifference and lack of attention, rejection by shouting, attributing blame to the child for problems, the transmission of negative messages that offend the dignity of the child, etc.

Emotional violence leaves a big mark on the victim. If it is longer lasting, it is more destructive than physical violence. Emotional violence is reflected in the permanent omission of expressing love and attention to children, as well as in verbal outbursts that humiliate and hurt children.

The forms of emotional abuse are: ignoring, rejecting, terrorizing, isolating and socializing, verbally injuring (belittling and insulting inappropriate terms - eg, a nerd, cattle, fat), verbal intimidation, attacking the most important values (beliefs, religions, races…) monitoring, tapping, eavesdropping on phone calls, etc.

Emotional abuse in a child victim creates confusion, causing the abuser to further abuse him. The goals of emotional abuse are to develop anxiety in the victim, to create dependence on the abuser, to weaken the physical and mental capacity to resist, provoking self-blame, etc. The most difficult form of emotional abuse is when the victim takes on the role of their abuser and begins to abuse herself, degrading herself.

It is clear that you have been through a lot, you have not really known yourself all your life and you have suffered many forms of abuse. Reading this book is your first step to recovery. The journey is long but the choice is yours and remember that even the longest journey begins with a simple step. If you have taken it, it means your journey has started and that is great.

Probably this brought back some bad memories, but as we wrote, it was not our intention. We intended to encourage you to learn and to break through the imaginary wall you created in your head. Most victims do this, almost always unconsciously, intending to forget bad memories and get away from problems. It's a good solution for a short time but causes problems in the long term. Denying and building walls only deepens and aggravates your mental state. So you have to go through this chapter to realize that you are not alone; that abuse is a phenomenon that affects many. It's not just children; unfortunately, abuse is a widespread phenomenon that affects all age groups. You had to go through all this again to break through that wall, to read about what you always held in denial.

In your case, it's a lot harder because the abuser was your mother and you were just a kid. You were incapable of understanding, you didn't understand why this was happening, you didn't know how to cope with abuse from the one person you love the most in the world.

You were ashamed, sad and you couldn't confide in anyone. You were afraid to open up to someone, even if that person was your closest friend. You were afraid to say that you were in pain, that you couldn't deal with it anymore. You didn't understand why, when you did everything right, instead of praising you would get taunting, yelling, and other humiliations.

But you have to snap out of it, you have to be strong. Because of this abuse that you have suffered, you have developed some behavioral patterns. These are just habits. You have become distrustful, pessimistic, unable to fit into the world. But this is just a defense mechanism that your mind has developed to protect yourself from what you see as a potential danger. Of course, you don't want to be hurt, you don't want to interact closely with people because you were hurt. Your behavioral patterns are created to protect you.

But these are just habits. Habits can be changed. Here you have to look at the whole problem like a true visionary. Only then will you be able to break through the great wall between you and the rest of the world.

That abuse formed your habits. Habits are part of automatic actions from our daily lives, even though we are sometimes not aware of them. They are like a hidden memory bank that tells us what to do. This is why Aristotle regards habits as "second nature" which brings us back to our "primary nature" or instinct. The difference is that habits are learned behaviors while instincts are innate. Habits allow us to perform multiple tasks at once and to do so efficiently and accurately. Because of this, a person can type and talk at the same time. This is because typing has become a common practice that does not require thinking to perform. This makes it easy for young people today to type a message on Twitter while simultaneously watching TV and talking with friends.

You should be brave in dealing with new situations. Get used to the unknown. Learn habits that will help you with the new circumstances. These may be similar to those you already have but should be adapted to your current assignment. A person playing basketball can easily switch to volleyball, as the habits developed in playing one sport can be transferred to another.

The study habits that researchers develop in their field can help them gain knowledge of other fields with less effort than individuals who have not developed these study habits. People can get used to expressing certain positive behaviors in different social situations, such as suppressing anger, showing solidarity and generosity. Indeed, some describe moral values as "ethical habits." These habits are a means by which people preserve the values of society as they prepare for what the future holds. They protect against the trauma of sudden changes. Habits allow people to learn quickly, respond with understanding, and effectively adapt to new developments. Past actions become an automatic response that requires no effort or attention, freeing the mind to deal with more important concerns.

Giordano Bruno was burned at the stake for opposing a geocentric view of space. Much later, Galileo was placed under house arrest for the same views. Many scientists faced hostility over proposing ideas that were contrary to what people knew. But innovative thinking is essential to discover. But what is essential in all of this is that habits can be changed. People can adapt their habits. Your defense can be transformed if you are willing to fight. That same habits will help you. But you must be persistent and you must break that wall, you simply must open your mind and think outside the box.

If they had not thought outside the box, Einstein would never have come up with a theory of relativity; Columbus would have never discovered America or Vasco de Gama discovered the Cape of Good Hope.

There's an old Native American proverb that talks about choice, or at least that's how we interpret it. The little Indian boy asked his father, "Dad, am I good or bad?" The father gazed in the distance and then looked at him and told him, "My son, in each of us there are two wolves, one wolf is good and the other evil." The little son then asked his father, "Well, which wolf prevails, Dad?" The father answered, "Son, the wolf we choose to feed prevails." So the choice is yours, you can either hide behind the victim mask or you can break those imaginary chains and be your own person. We know you will make the right decision.

CHAPTER FIVE: TYPICAL BEHAVIOR OF A CHILD WITH A BORDERLINE MOTHER

We have come to the part of the book where you will be able to see how children with borderline mothers behave.

A large number of children who have undergone this type of trauma exhibit different patterns of behavior but there are common traits to them all children. As a child of a borderline mother, you only see the world in two colors, unfortunately. You see the world in white and black. You have to know that the world has many colors. A variation of black and white can only create gray. A gray world is not a place for you and it is not a place for other children. The voice that wakes you up and tells you that you are small, that you are not worthy, that others are better, is wrong. Tell it to leave.

One day you will wake up and realize that there is no more time to do the things you have always wanted to do. You will indulge in that annoying little voice and let him beat you. So immediately tell him to leave. Do it now and continue reading this book and looking for answers. Remember, the answers are there, you may just need to dig a little deeper. They are hidden as obvious truths and they can be learned by those who want to know them so much that they are ready to dig. This book is, therefore, a great step for you.

You are now thinking that you are safe where you are and you are afraid to go further because you think that if you stay where you are, there will be no pain. In a way you are right, there really will be nothing. But not in a good way. You will be on the bad side of this story, you will not move anywhere and you will stay in one place forever.

You will be simply stuck. A ship is safest when it is in port, but the ship is not made to be in port. The ship was built to sail, to move away from the shore and go on to the open sea. A motionless ship will never help people and eventually, the rust will do its thing and the ship will perish even though it never set sail. The same thing applies to people. Your open sea awaits you. New people are waiting to come into your life. People who can give a lot and who will give love to you.

Even though you may not be aware, you are already walking towards the answers. Reading this book will reveal to you the truths that have always been distant to you and that you thought were hidden. They were never hidden, but you were afraid to ask; you were afraid because of everything you went through. To see that you are not alone, we will show you how children behave when abused by mothers with Borderline Personality Disorder.

The baby is small and innocent and the earliest attachment should be just with the mother. This is the main problem. When a mother is suffering from Borderline Personality Disorder, this bonding between mother and child does not go well. So from the very beginning of your life, just like many other children, the problem arose immediately.

5.1. Children who are abused by their mother with Borderline Personality Disorder vs other abused children.

Borderline Personality Disorder is such an insidious condition that it leaves children who have been abused in such relationships with specific problems. Mothers with Borderline Personality Disorders initially show much less desire to connect with their children. They are cooler from the start, distant, and less concerned about their children.

Such mothers provide much less smiles and much less play for their children, they do not touch them and there is no integration.

To make matters worse, mothers with Borderline Personality Disorders often have a problem identifying their child's emotions and responding appropriately to the child's needs. This deprives the child of safety, comfort, and the security needed at the beginning of life.

 How can you grow up and become more social and eager to get to know yourself and the world around when you there were completely different problems for you to face at home? You had no compassion because your mother couldn't give it to you. Remember this, your mother was ill. You were drawn into abuse without the will of the abuser. There was no conscious reaction and desire to abuse.

The general types of abuse can vary and the abuse itself can be mental, physical and even sexual. Some children suffered more than you and some of them less. But there are two big differences between deliberate abuse and the abuse that comes from a mother with BPD. The first difference is that these children are abused with intention. So the abuser wanted them to suffer. It can be a comfort to you that you were not abused because your mother wanted to abuse you. Her actions and anger towards you were not intended to hurt you. She hurt you a lot, but she didn't want to and you have to understand that. She deeply loved you but couldn't show that because of her condition. Her sadness, anger, and frustration were not created by her desire but by her impulses. Because of this, you have to forgive her; you will realize in time that she never wanted you to suffer.

 The other difference is that, because of the complexity of the situation, you are hurt much more deeply than other children who have been deliberately abused. Unfortunately, you have had constant abuse and with far greater consequences because you have never been able to get answers for your questions and have never been able to connect with your mother in the right way.

5.2. Your behavior

You likely act antisocially, are distrustful and have an "always on the lookout" attitude. It's your defense mechanism. As a young child, you wanted answers and couldn't find them because your behavioral mechanism was not set up properly. As parents pass their behavior on to children, so do children form their personality because it is a natural process. You lacked those emotions and now you don't know how to approach a person properly. As a kid, you always looked to lean away so someone else wouldn't hurt you. That's why we compared you to a ship standing in the harbor. You've never had a real interaction and it's the same as a ship that has never sailed. As you grew, you grew further away from people, maybe you hid behind a hobby to fool yourself into thinking you did not have a problem. You didn't interfere too much in human relationships and didn't talk much. You felt that your opinion didn't matter and that nobody cared because you developed a sense of being of less value. Deep down, you were afraid of being hurt. That's why you run from reality to imagination. You created the world within yourself and you put a wall around it. In that world, there was only room for trying to close the emotional hole that had arisen. You've probably tried music, writing, painting or just fantasizing. Later, you began to fear love because you never got any. You refused any loving relationship because you saw your mother and that close relationship in all things and it reminded you of her. You were afraid that if you embarked on another relationship that required closeness, you would again feel like you were a little helpless child. That's why you broke up or ran away from them.

You still feel the same today. You're scared of people. You are afraid of interaction in every way. That's why you're in a vicious circle and you can't get out of it. We tell you, you can. You are in a vicious circle and inside a big wall. It's time to tear down that wall and move on.

5.3. *The consequences of the abuse itself*

Childhood abuse has an impact on five significant, interconnected areas: neurological and intellectual development; school success and life expectancy; socio-emotional development; social relations and behavior; mental health as a whole. In each of these areas, the consequences can be immediate and/or long-term. Abuse and neglect in most cases happens to children repeatedly, and the consequences depend on the age of the child – the victim. In terms of socio-emotional development, decreased self-control, increased dependence on other people, depression, lower self-esteem and a sense of inability to control life events occur. Social skills and social perceptions are poorly developed in the area of social relations.

5.4. *Aggression*

Aggression is always there because you are deeply angry with yourself that you cannot do better and that you know your life is passing by and you are helplessly watching. Your frustration and anger turns into aggression because aggression is your pressure valve.

Aggression and delinquency, psychosomatic disorders (allergy, asthma, and indigestion) occur. Children develop various defense and adjustment mechanisms: dissociation (denial and repression of feelings and events), self-blame, idealization of the abusive parent (resulting from the fragmentation that leads to the inability to evaluate themselves and others) and self-destructive behavior (self-harm, alcohol, drug use, sexual risk behavior).

5.5. Panic

Panic is something that is also your companion. Children who grew up with a mother who has Borderline Personality Disorder often feel panic and anxiety. It's a side effect of the fear you have come to expect.

Feelings of discomfort, anxiety, fear, hopelessness, confusion, loneliness, and anxiety are also prevalent. Post-traumatic stress reactions may occur. The long-term consequences of the abuse are difficulties concerning fundamental trust in others, independence, and personal effectiveness. Men often become abusers of their partners and their children, while women enter into partnerships in which they act as victims and may abuse the children. Most research has addressed the characteristics of abusive parents with BPD. Parents who were abused in 30-40% of cases were found to be abusing their children. An intergenerational chain of abuse is not necessary if the child has received, with a realistic experience of parenting behavior, sufficient social and emotional support from the wider and immediate environment.

5.6. You don't have a complete personality

You're not whole. You feel that deep inside. You know you're missing something. You need something else to be whole. You tried to find yourself in other people. You tried to imitate others because you don't want to be you. He would rather be anyone else. This is because you do not love yourself and do not believe in yourself.

Studies have shown that child neglect can be more pernicious than outright abuse, and that neglected toddlers fall into the most vulnerable category: the most anxious, careless and apathetic, distrustful, withdrawn, insensitive to grief and potentially aggressive. Children who are actively denied parental love and attention develop a labile ego structure, later susceptible to psychic crisis or breakdown. A retrospective analysis of individual cases indicates that childhood neglect, which occurs in early childhood, increases the likelihood of severe depression later. Children of mothers with BPD, who have not learned to create a warm and safe climate in the family, immediately after birth, develop an insecure parental attachment relationship.

5.7. Your mother didn't even know what she wanted from you

Your mother suffered a great deal in herself. And there were times when she wasn't aware of it. It's scary and sad. She didn't know what was real and she couldn't define herself, and you went into this whole story to be her valve and that is what caused your present behavior.

Such mothers are often unrealistic when it comes to what they expect from their children, and if the child's individual growth does not match the mothers' egoistic aspirations, the frustrations and feelings of parental failure can lead to abuse. In this case, children are faced with painful stages of adaptation to stress, which is reflected in their emotional and social growth and development. In later life, these result in difficulties concerning others, as they tend to expect abuse and destruction in every object relationship, become insecure, closed to new experiences and new acquaintances, less curious and less willing to learn from their peers. According to statistics, abused children have difficulty mastering school materials, and about 65 percent of these children repeat the first grade.

5.8. Feelings of guilt

You're just a victim. You are the one who is not guilty, the one who is innocent. If we look at this situation more broadly, we will find that conditionally speaking, it is difficult to see the culprit. If you are looking for a culprit and resent your mother, we will tell you right away, the culprit is your mother's condition; the culprit is not your mother. However, to make matters worse, you are the one who has developed a sense of guilt and shame. You feel guilty because you think that you have caused this behavior of your mother. Now we tell you to stop it, don't condemn yourself because you are not guilty. You have nothing to be ashamed of. Just think; is it logical to be ashamed? How logical, if you think a little better, is it to be ashamed that in some ways life was not fair to you and your mother? You feel ashamed to share it with someone, but if you were to share it, you would not get mockery but compassion. Think of it this way, you didn't write a petition for someone to give birth to you, you didn't write a petition to come into this world, you couldn't choose where you were going to be born, who you were going to grow up with. Does it seem clearer to you now why must open yourself up?

A victim who has experienced recurrent traumas of childhood abuse by a BPD mother feels guilty, ashamed, fearful and distrustful, is insecure and hesitant in decision making and has a sense of personal lack, and as she loses her sense of worth, is socially isolated from other family members and society.

Because children are the best imitators of their parents, long-term abuse in an atmosphere of broken marital and family relationships negatively targets them – that violence is effective and is an acceptable way of resolving conflict. As they grow up, these children can become rude spouses and parents who often abuse their partners and their sons and daughters. Galdston (1979) states that one who has long been exposed to physical abuse in childhood can become a person who practices sadomasochistic sexual acts concerning a partner. The abuse that takes place in the family environment of deeply disturbed relationships, pervasive fear and totalitarian control, seduced by violence, threats, and punishment, leads to the child feeling helpless and seeing greater harm in himself than in the abuse itself (Herman, 1996).

5.9. Consequences of abuse - drugs and alcohol

You don't like reality. You are disgusted with reality. You hate the image of this world and yourself in it and that's why you need to change reality. The distortion of reality is easiest if you put yourself in a state where you will lose that line between reality and imagination. It's a very thin line. Unfortunately, imagination and reality are most easily combined through the abuse of alcohol and drugs. If you have tried this way to ease the pain it is not difficult to understand why this is so. However, you are likely well aware that when the effects of opiates cease, all problems return and start hitting you like a freight train. You are only destroying your health, and problems remain. The key to the solution is hidden and lies in having the courage to face your problems. You must know that you can do this and that by talking about your problems, you will find the help you need to be a fully functional person and have a good and fulfilling life.

Mental health facilities and psychological counseling centers are full of people who have endured long-term, recurrent trauma in childhood. Research shows that abused children can meet diagnostic criteria for disorders such as addiction and substance abuse (alcohol and other psychoactive substances), personality disorder, various types of phobias, anxiety, post-traumatic stress disorder (which can lead to permanent personality changes), dissociative disorder, eating disorders (anorexia and bulimia), suicidal behavior, and even the most severe psychiatric disorder – psychosis. Much more often than their other peers, such children appear as delinquents, being potential perpetrators of rape, robbery, crime, and other misdemeanors. From all of the above, it can be concluded that childhood trauma impairs the achievement of developmental goals and tasks, and the lasting consequences it leaves leads to long-term psychological trauma. A BPD mother's relationship can have a very adverse effect on all aspects of an individual's life.

5.10. You have become skeptical about life itself

It's quite understandable that many children in such a situation may become very skeptical of life. This is not surprising because the simple fact is that, metaphorically, you have not been dealt good cards. Life has played with you, but stop wasting your time looking at those cards. Time passes as you analyze them. Instead, try to play the best you can with those cards.

Such children can become moody, irritable, and resentful, can seem exhausted and be withdrawn. In contact with family, peers, and friends, they can become aggressive. However, children who are merely innocent bystanders of such violence can also suffer the consequences. This causes them great fear, which causes their ability to learn to decline, so they can also become potential victims of various types of social predators.

Life does not ask you to be the best, but it asks you to do your best. So never give up because there is always a place when the tide will change. That is why, like the boat we mentioned, you must sail into life.

CHAPTER SIX: WHICH MASK ARE YOU WEARING – THE CONSEQUENCES IN ADULTHOOD

We'll start this chapter with a trivial question. Ever wondered why superheroes wear masks? Superheroes wear masks to hide their identities, hence to protect themselves. And you probably put on a mask too. But there is a difference between you and them. Superheroes invent identities to defend the costume. And you? You invented a costume to defend your identity.

Imagine dividing the world into people who love the color red and people who love the color blue. There is no intermediate space, there are no other colors. You divide yourself to see the world in just these colors.

6.1. Colors are important

But there are so many colors out there. We know that there are not only red and blue colors; we actually have a wide variety of colors and it is also possible to love multiple colors at once. The same thing applies to people. The world is not just black and white, and therefore neither are we. There are indeed 50 shades of gray. This is not to say that we all suffer from Borderline Personality Disorder, but rather that we can be different depending on the situation itself, the people we associate with, and our needs at any given time. The different faces, or masks, we portray represent our different versions of ourselves. They represent our capacity for adaptation, which is the only constant in a changing world.

6.2. How does your face develop and what does it mask?

Putting on a mask is, unfortunately, a side effect of your trauma. You created that mask because you think that you will be protected from possible abuse. You simply choose to hide and we understand why. Your mask was a necessity for you because you didn't want to reveal yourself to others. The fear of hurting was and still is, too great. But you must take off your mask. Your identity isn't something you need to hide. That mask is preventing you from having a close relationship with anyone and the sad truth is that the mask is destroying you, so take it off.

Why?

In childhood, we are like unformed clay. You can often hear people mourn their childhood because at that time they felt most like their true selves. During this period we are what we are at our core and we act that way. Children act following their feelings and needs. They have no inhibitions. As we grow up and become aware of other people, others' expectations, and our own, we develop the need to belong, to fit in and to protect ourselves. We change and a greater number of our selves emerge. The experience shapes our faces, to enable us to cope with the world in the best and most adaptable way.

6.3. The endless loophole

Life presents us with an everyday masquerade in which we wear a different suit depending on where we are going. The masks are similar. Our experiences play a large role in the emergence of our masks. From it, we gain a picture of ourselves and how the world sees us. Masks often arise as a product of seeing some of our weaknesses and the need to replace that weakness with something better. Unlike our different faces, that have their essence in ourselves, the mask is an artificial creation, without the material that exists in us; something we make from other people's material to replace the parts of ourselves that we do not love. It can be seen as a form of compensation; we compensate for our shortcomings by adopting certain traits and abilities that manage to cover those cracks we found in ourselves. But, unlike compensation, where the acquisition of skills and abilities represents a certain development of ourselves, the masks do not have that developmental direction, they do not represent mastering new skills but pretending to possess those skills or pretending to think in a certain way all to escape from what we are. That is why a mask is worthless and you are mistaken by wearing the mask.

6.4. A school example

Do you remember yourself in adolescence, when the need for belonging and acceptance was the strongest? You may have become a fan of cars or heavy metal music overnight, just because these were things that interested your peers. You put on the masks of a girlfriend or guy who didn't mind anything in a relationship, just so someone wouldn't leave you. And all that had its purpose. In adulthood, through additional experiences, deeper relationships, and a deeper knowledge of ourselves and the world, you become great at masking your true self. The masquerade of life has a practical application, because there are times when we do need to adapt to our surroundings. The question is, what happens when we no longer recognize we are wearing the mask?

6.5. The mask is not real

Ever since the beginnings of the world, masks have been created by people like you; people who felt that their personality wasn't complete. You hide behind someone else, but you know that is not you.

6.6. Let's go back a little

Long ago, when going to war, warriors dressed in special costumes, and smeared colors on their faces. Such behavior aimed to make warriors from ordinary workers, citizens. To accomplish their task, to go to battle, they had to become someone else, someone they probably hadn't been before. Today, we don't have to go quite that far; but we could consider makeup as a similar preparation for battle with the world. But what is the point of it? In a new situation, when we do not know what awaits us, putting color on our face is a shield for us – just as knights had shields, so today we use masks to protect ourselves.

6.7. What are you protecting?

You wear a mask to protect your ego, but also that child's uninhibited part of yourself, your true identity, because the world is not only your playground, it is the playground of all people and no one is guaranteed comfort and safety. Look at all the superheroes hiding behind the mask. Their initial experiences were not great, they were hurt, weak, they did not like how others saw them, or how they saw themselves. And then they would put on a costume, put on a mask and become someone else, someone better, stronger, faster – heroes. It is the same with you. You put on your warrior colors when facing the world, to lift yourself up, to pat yourself on the back and to say "I can do it."

But now is the time to forget about the mask. We know that you adopted the mask, because thanks to it, you do not stay in bed every day thinking that the world is sad and ugly. However, that is not the answer.

6.8. Why are you hiding?

The mask represents an escape from reality, and with that escape comes problems of identity and acceptance of oneself, which results in dissatisfaction with life. Prolonged use of the mask leads to a loss of health. In addition to the feelings of loneliness it creates, the mask makes it impossible for us to connect with another person. It isolates us, even though it may have once been a function of actually bringing us closer and attracting people. Think of a school bully. Psychology tells us that in many cases the aggressive behavior of such children is a mask and that they feel smaller than poppy seeds. They use that mask of a bully to protect themselves and to gain a sense of power that they lack.

But in adulthood, when that mask is easily translucent or when aggression no longer leads to the status of strength but is rather seen as something bad, that mask creates more problems than benefits. The mask loses its adaptability, and the person who has been using it for so long faces a crisis where she is required to redefine her understanding of herself and what is expected of her, as well as the mechanisms she has used to meet her needs. Changing such content is not easy, and often people don't even try, but rather bang their heads against the wall hoping that it will break the wall rather than their head.

6.9. Why do we protect our masks?

As we said, we wear masks to protect our ego, and our true personality. But if you continue to do so, eventually, your true personality will fade. You will become that mask and you will forget who you really are. That is why you need to throw that mask away and start to rebuild yourself. This is one of the most important things that you must do to help yourself.

6.10. Masked love – another example

When do we hide from the world? When we think we are not good enough or when we think we are not worthy. We all use masks from time to time, not because we are corrupt and insincere, but because we want to be loved and allowed to love. In the early days of your relationship, you may have shared everything your partner likes, only to slowly relax over time and allow yourself to be different because you felt comfortable enough to show him that you had different interests without fear of rejection. Why do we do this? Why don't we immediately say, "I'm weird about chocolate, I don't like to share." Because we want to be loved by that person, we want to hold that image of the ideal for as long as possible. It has its function, it allows us to see each other a second time, a third and a fourth, and so on until the time when more masks are not so necessary and it is okay to show your face.

6.11. Identity crisis

Our different versions of ourselves, our faces, all exist at the same moment, but they do not all occur at once. There is cognitive processing of the situation and an assessment of which version is now appropriate. In addition to how our brains work in such a complex way, the priority you give to a particular version or a certain understanding of yourself influences when which version will appear to you.

The fear of loneliness and the need to be loved pushes us to the brink of our capabilities and willingness to use whatever means we can think of to fulfill our goals and needs. One would think that, from so many versions and faces, our system would overheat and explode, but, the more complex you are as a person, the more different you are – the more peaceful you are.

The mask and faces are not the same. The mask is an artificial creation, and the face is a part of us - not the separate part we put on when we go to fight criminals. Masks are not necessarily bad for our health, they have an adaptive role as our faces, it is only a matter of assessing to what extent it is useful to have a mask, and when it is better to show your face. In your case, it is time to show your face to the world.

6.12. You don't need to be someone else

Every day we learn something new about ourselves and the world. And with that, our color palette is expanding. Think of it as having an endless stack of cards and constantly pulling out a new card for a new situation. And for each new situation, we might craft a new version of ourselves. Consider the many different faces you exhibit throughout your life: the person who jumped over the kindergarten fence with their childhood companion and swung in the middle of the night on a swing, and the one who diligently goes to college and listens with serious facial expressions is the same person, as is the one who goes to work to do responsible and sometimes daunting work. And while it is the goal to seek the true version of ourselves, you must accept the existence of all those versions and to develop a sense of wholeness. Because with that feeling that you are one whole, not separate parts; you will be able to feel fulfilled and, without feeling guilty or divided, at every opportunity will actually be you and not someone else. The mask is a defensive mechanism, nothing more. You suffered a lot and you needed a mask, but now your identity is at stake, you must protect you. Don't hide in the dark, you need light to heal. You need your identity back.

CHAPTER SEVEN: LEARN HOW TO DEFEND YOURSELF AGAINST THEM

N ormal and disruptive are two concepts that are never clearly demarcated. It is difficult to determine where one begins and the other ends. The most common issues when it comes to mental health are realism, self-control, self-esteem, the ability to have close relationships, and the desire for self-realization.

People with Borderline Personality Disorder suffering from anxiety, loss of touch with reality, depression, among other symptoms. Treatment involves therapy, which may include medication or psychotherapy, which involves verbal and/or non-verbal communication.

7.1. About everything

Mental disorders can occur in people of all professions, classes and cultures. Race, gender, money, and socio-economic background do not prevent or cause mental illness. This is why your mother also has this condition.

What is most important to you is to learn how to behave properly with your mother. This is very important because if you do not learn how to behave well with a mother who because of her condition has great problems, the damage in your relationship will be increased. But you also need to understand that it's important to build a defense mechanism. You have to learn to defend yourself and somehow balance yourself in this difficult situation.

We know that you feel anger and that it is not easy for you; we know that great damage has been done and that you have no more desire to be anyone's valve. You were a victim and you carry your scars with you. But you have to learn how to defend yourself. This way you will protect both yourself and your mother. Remember that your mental health is the most important thing and only if you are completely healthy and protected you can help your mother and yourself.

7.2. How to approach this problem

The most important thing is to try never to argue with your mother. You have to learn to restrain yourself and ask questions slowly and meaningfully because only in this way will you be able to defend yourself.

7.3. Specific examples

We think it's best to start by showing you some specific examples of conversation. That way you will be able to understand how you need to put yourself in this situation and learn to defend yourself. In most cases, this is not at all easy.

This is the basic thing to know when it comes how to help your mother suffering from a mental illness such as Borderline Personality Disorder. When talking to your mother, you have to act this way.

What you want to say: "Can't you see that you need serious help?"

What you should say instead: "Do you agree that you have been sleeping badly lately? Maybe we should make an appointment with a doctor. You want me to call him?"

It's not uncommon for people who are sick to be completely unaware of it. People who do not want help often refuse good advice. Therefore, starting from what they are aware of is a good start.

Below is another example. We hope that through concrete examples you will best understand how to successfully and positively interact with your mother.

7.4. Example

What you mean: "Did you take the medicine? Did you take the medicine? Did you take the medicine?"

What you should say instead: "Do you want me to help you organize your medicine box so you know when and what to take?"

You must never feed on your mothers addiction, her depression, or her aggression. You must never start arguing or let your her see your own aggression because she is ill, remember that. Any of your behaviors that she takes as an invitation to a quarrel will cause her to react badly, and again you will suffer more because of it.

7.5. Here is another specific example

What you mean: "You have no reason to be depressed!"

What you should say instead: "If you and your psychiatrist agree, I'd love to attend one of your conversations to better understand what's bothering you."

Even if the river of pain is pouring from you and you want to blame her, you must not show that aggression. That is why you should take this approach in such cases.

7.6. Another example

What you want to say: "Snap out of it!"

What you should say instead: "It's not always going to be this way."

Giving hope is your priority, especially for someone suffering from depression. When it comes to depression, the patient believes that it will last forever. During those dark moments, you must be optimistic and supportive. This does not mean that you should be a psychiatrist to your mother, but you can encourage her and help her accept the fact that you are not her enemy. Show her that you understand her. It will develop some kind of empathy within her and your relationship will become much better.

7.7. Understand the nature of mental illness

Mentally illness can be difficult to understand by those who have not experienced it. It is much easier for many of us to learn how to deal with irrational delusions, fear, hallucinations, and sadness than with irrational anger.

Mental illness can be frightening when we witness it in our loved one, particularly when a person with a disorder of consciousness screams and gestures as though they are preparing to attack. In every situation, the possibility of violence must be objectively assessed. If your mother shows signs of aggression, never feed that aggression. We know it's very difficult, but you have to do it for yourself and your mother.

7.8. The optimal approach for you

First of all, you need to control your emotional attitude. If you are both tense, go to different places first and calm down. At least try to relax. Here are some tips:

- Count slowly to 10;

- Breathe deeply and slowly;

- Walk (around the room, down the street);

- Try something else positive and enjoyable;

- Take a break (do something around the house).

The situation is easier to control, with clear and calm behavior. Communication is very important when emotions heighten. A mentally ill mother needs you to express confidence. Often, a firm and soothing voice allows you to quickly dispel your mother's irrational feelings. Remember that behind anger and confusion, there is often internal trouble and fear lurking.

7.9. Give your mother space, be careful and safe

When communicating with an angry person, you must be present. You shouldn't be hugging her, but you have to be there. Do not block the exit from the room, but stand so that in the event of an emergency you have the opportunity to move away. When a mentally ill person is disturbed, beware of any contact if you are not entirely sure that she will like it.

As your mother's anger is usually caused by a specific event, be as careful as possible with her. Gently try to discover the source of the anger. Do not ignore or minimize the alarm. Help your mother focus on what will help her cool her anger. Initially, it is necessary to find a way to calm down and later, in a calm state, to find out the cause of the anger.

Do not allow your mother to cross the line of acceptable behavior. If she raises her voice, throws things, threatens you, breaks furniture, or worries neighbors, you must confidently object and say that this is bad behavior.

7.10. Basic rules for combating a BPD mother's anger:

- Do not lose your composure, speak calmly and clearly;

- Stay calm, do not show your fear, as this will only make the situation worse;

- Give her the opportunity to leave;

- Do not touch or approach your mother until she has approved it;

- Try to objectively evaluate the possible outcome;

- Try to determine how angry and unreasonable she is, whether it is a manifestation of the disease or if there is another reason to consider;

- Do not discuss nonsensical ideas;

- Help her decide on further action;

- Protect yourself and others from possible violence.

If irritation and anger are common components of your mother's behavior, and she regularly releases aggression, then wait for the anger to pass, before attempting to discuss the matter wth her.

7.11. *You need to follow these four rules:*

1. Do not irritate your mother, as this will cause even more aggression.
2. Unleash your negative energy through workouts, chores, or just go and yell out in a hidden place.
3. Calm yourself by watching television or reading a book.
4. Give your mother medication prescribed by a doctor.

To reduce the likelihood of repeated anger attacks, you must first understand that a mentally ill person is an ordinary person with characteristics such as self-doubt and low self-esteem. Treat your mother with understanding; like any sick person, she needs compassion and support. A mentally ill mother is also disorganized physiologically and spiritually. You don't have to scold her for that; try to communicate more optimistically, put kindness, warmth, and respect into the conversation.

7.12. *Things you must never forget*

Remember that someone suffering from a mental disorder may get confused, and their feelings and contradictions increase. If your mother does not turn to anger, you must communicate with her more often about the problems and difficulties she encounters. There is no need for long conversations; speak slowly and clearly. Let your mother be alone, take a break from others. If the situation gets out of hand, call an ambulance or police immediately.

7.13. What else do you need to know?

The medical definition of Borderline Personality Disorder tells us that it is a mental illness that is mainly characterized by a disorder of attitude towards reality, a disorder of thought, sensory deception, and a disorder of emotional expression. These symptoms can appear either individually or in different combinations. In the initial stages of the disease's development, intellectual ability is maintained, although over time certain cognitive deficits may develop. The disorder affects the basic functions of behavior.

Such a person may consider her most intimate thoughts, feelings or actions to be known by others and in this connection may develop delusional interpretations in the sense that natural or unnatural forces influence her thoughts and actions, often in a bizarre way. Thoughts are often dominated by peripheral and irrelevant concepts that are otherwise inhibited in normal mental activity.

Borderline Personality Disorder is caused by imbalances in the metabolism of the so-called neurotransmitters found in certain brain regions. The mechanism of neurotransmitter operation could most simply be illustrated as a fast data flow between two nerve endings. In this way, the two endings are in communication with each other, and as a result of a large number of such neural connections, total brain function is created. The metabolism of these substances is very lively and precisely regulated, and a certain disturbance in their metabolism is the cause of the condition.

Current knowledge indicates that there is multifactorial causation in the onset of psychosis, and we know from this that the disease is not only hereditary or genetically determined, since in only 48% of cases of identical twins do both members suffer from this condition. The disorder is not sampled solely by environmental factors, and we can say that the condition is caused by genetic predisposition, and in combination with environmental factors.

Borderline Personality Disorder is not a product of desire, insolence, or inactivity. Factors that increase the likelihood of psychosis are a genetic predisposition and accumulated stress events, and excessive alcohol and drug use.

7.14. What does all of this mean?

This means that Borderline Personality Disorder is one of the most complex conditions and this can have catastrophic consequences. So you have to direct your behavior as we showed you in the examples. Don't yell, don't show aggression, and try as hard as you can to support your mother. We know that you feel angry, but remember that everything you went through was just a result of your mother's condition. If you want to help yourself you have to help her too. Only in this way, will you help yourself. Forgive all the insults and all the humiliation. Let the knowledge that your mother didn't want this help you. These are all just life circumstances and for you to learn how to treat your mother and defend yourself properly you must accept that. This way you will be able to move on and have a good and healthy life.

CHAPTER EIGHT: HOW TO HELP A CHILD COPE WITH A BORDERLINE MOTHER

Many things have been taken from you; we will not pretend that is not the case. You have been thrown into the mud from the very beginning of your life and your life circumstances have forced you to become a person who is afraid of interaction. They have caused you to become a person wearing a mask, a person who does not trust others and who thinks that he is not good enough for others.

You have had many challenges throughout your life, you have suffered a lot. There was never enough attention, love, compassion, and tenderness for you. You as a child needed to be loved. You were loved, but you were also distressed due to life circumstances. As a kid you needed love, you needed attention, you needed a hand you could take. You needed a foothold in life.

Unfortunately, you didn't get any of this. From birth you were thrown into a whirlwind of aggression and you could never understand why this was so. We have talked about everything you went through. But one thing is clear and worthy of note – you are still here, you are reading this because deep down you know that you can bring your life back, that you can live better and you have made your decision. You deserve a medal because you didn't give up, you didn't let that stop you, you moved on. Everything that life threw into your face, you threw back at life, put simply, you managed to defend yourself.

8.1. How to deal with a mother suffering from Borderline Personality Disorder

In this story, children are the main victims because they need help and they should not have to pay for what is not their fault. If we look at all this objectively, we can see it is not their mother's fault either but the fault of fate. Many children suffer daily and should be motivated by what you have gone through and what you have overcome. And one more thing is very important; who is a better person than you to understand the pain and suffering of other children who are going through life with a mother with Borderline Personality Disorder?

Your "friends in pain", the children who have been through the same abuse as you are experiencing social anxiety.

8.2. What is social anxiety?

When children experience social anxiety, they are afraid of situations where they have to interact with other people, and they are afraid of situations where they would be the center of attention. They are often worried that others will think badly about them or that they will do something shameful.

Social anxiety is mainly seen in older children and teenagers but can be diagnosed even in children as young as four. It occurs as a consequence of poor relationships between children and mothers.

Some of the signs of social anxiety in children are:

- They are shy or withdrawn;
- They have difficulty approaching other children or joining groups;
- They have a limited number of friends;

- They tend to avoid situations where they notice that they might be the focus (such as not wanting to start a game even when the teacher asks for it; not answering questions in front of other children, etc.).

8.3. They think bad things will happen

School children with social anxiety usually have a fear of reading aloud in front of the class or answering questions in front of others. Sometimes they start avoiding daily activities such as going to school (feigning illness, etc.). School children avoid or rarely perform in front of peers or seniors. They often have a worse concentration than other children. Also, it is not uncommon for them to avoid birthday parties or visiting friends; they rarely initiate the first game or call to go to the park. Young children have a fear of new things, are irritable and cry often, they refuse to speak, and often withdraw from the group.

Some children with social anxiety monitor group events very closely, but never join in. Children with anxiety lack the confidence to try new things, and sometimes they are unable to cope with daily challenges. Some anxious children are prone to angry outbursts.

As with adults, social anxiety in children can also have physical symptoms such as nausea, abdominal pain, redness, hand tremors, and the like. It is not easy to notice social anxiety at this age. The reason for this is because children are small and often obedient to institutions (which is a desirable situation, right?), so perhaps less attention is paid to something that "doesn't look like a problem." Also, children may not be able to talk about it. In most cases, younger children do not have a well-developed set of words to explain what is happening to them, what they are afraid of, and what they are worried about.

8.4. Shame or social anxiety

Shyness is not a problem itself; many shy children make satisfying, long-term friendships. But the problem occurs when it prevents a child from engaging in daily activities such as class discussions with older children or fun events with kindergarten children, or making lasting friendships along the way. In this case, the problem must be resolved.

How can we help a child who has a social anxiety issue because of their mother's influence?

There are many things you can do at home with your children, or when you are in another social setting, or whenever you talk to them about their disturbing emotions.

At home (by father or family member):

Try to prepare your child for situations that are scary or worrying. Act out the situation in the house and practice things that would make it easier for him/her in their next encounter with the unwanted situation. Encourage your child to do some "detective work." For example, if he thinks everyone will laugh at him if he answers the questions asked in a class or kindergarten, ask "how do you know that someone will laugh at you?" It can also help to talk to your child about some of the times when you, too, felt anxious in social situations. This can help your child feel that it is perfectly okay to talk about how he or she feels. They will consider it supportive. Gently encourage your child to join a particular social situation and start new activities. Assess the situation yourself but try to avoid ones that can make the problem worse;

Do not force your child to talk or do things in front of others unless he or she wants to. If your child has an anxious reaction to this situation, do not immediately lose patience, but try a second time with a little more preparation. Do not punish your child for "failure" or push him or her into any given situation.

Inform the teacher of your child's anxiety problem. It is also important to note what you all do at home with your child to address social anxiety. In this way, educators can get involved in the problem and there is the possibility that they will try to provide the child with consistent support as much as possible.

When talking to your child:

Whenever your child completes an activity he or she found frightening, let them know that you think they are brave. Praise him quietly and when you are on your own; make it a very important thing that he has been able to accomplish this task. This helps to nurture children's self-esteem.

Avoid labeling your child as "shy." If others comment on your child's behavior in social situations and front of him/her, you can always respond "he relaxes with people he knows well." Even if you feel frustrated, avoid criticizing the child or displaying any negative behavior related to their social anxiety.

8.5. Kids need help

You know what social anxiety is. You went through all this yourself. All that you have gone through, the abuse and lack of support you received led to symptoms that can be called one general and abstract name – social anxiety.

8.6. Hard life

Much is said about violence; what happened, who committed it and who suffered from it. Society is often urged to report every form of violence as soon as it is encountered, but do we know how to recognize a victim of violence? How do we recognize a child who lives with a mother suffering from Borderline Personality Disorder? And how do we help him or her cope?

8.7. What is violence?

We all know what physical violence is – bruises, torn skin, and hiding injuries. But it is important to know that violence does not have to be physical.

Violence can also include calling someone derogatory names, insulting, ridiculing, intimidating, mocking, expelling from a group, spreading rumors, ordering, cruel criticism and blackmailing.

Psychological violence can be brutal and can cause a child to lose faith in himself completely. Victims are afraid to seek new friends for fear of being rejected again, so they choose to be alone, withdrawing into themselves.

The younger the child, the more likely it is that nightmarish fears, urination, stuttering and sucking of the thumb will occur as a result of the abuse, so extra attention should be paid to this, whether it is happening to your child or a child in your area. Older children experience self-harm – suicidal thoughts occur, and the parent may notice that the child is beginning to lie, as well as developing alcohol and drug problems.

Although victims are mostly withdrawn, silent and submissive, there is a possibility that the consequences of the abuse may be manifested differently. The victim may lose her sense of empathy for others and become a bully herself. Victims experience aggression, and the child usually tries to make up for the loss of control and helplessness by responding with aggression of her own.

8.8. Silence is a problem

Children often choose to remain silent, and violence can be difficult to prove. Children are silent and suffering, and any long-term stress has serious health and psychological consequences. Eating and sleeping disorders occur, and it can be observed that children have frequent headaches and abdominal pain. When a child suffers from violence, extreme and frequent mood swings, changes in habit, and low self-esteem can occur. The victims remain silent and fear that if they admit they have been abused and abused, it will be worse. The children fear that the abuser, in this case, the mother, will find out and become even more brutal. It is important to teach children that there is no excuse for violence. No one should endanger one's right to a dignified life, no matter who it is.

8.9. A no-win situation - what's going on in the victim's head?

Violence emotionally disables a child, creating a feeling of helplessness, hopelessness or despair. Violence can make children believe that they will never escape the clutches of the abuser. Victims can often be identified by a constant state of alertness, to the point that they are never fully relaxed, and are jumping at every sound. Victims have difficulties in social relationships; suffer from social anxiety, tension, and depression, which can continue to be expressed throughout life.

8.10. These are children's jobs

As stated above, victims of violence feel guilty and live in fear. If a child happens to trust you, do not let him down, accuse him of lying, or tell him that the problem will be solved by itself, but rather do your best to help him.

If you suspect that a child has been abused, broach this issue indirectly to gain the child's confidence. Avoid statements that start with "You," as they may indicate in the child's head that they are wrong.

Also, pay attention to the tone you in which you are addressing your child. If you are too serious, she may give you the answers she thinks you want to hear. Speak in a more relaxed tone, which will encourage the child to reveal all the details.

8.11. How to deal

A child abused by their mother is the most difficult category of abuse when it comes to getting them to talk, because of the deep love children have for their mother. But children should be encouraged in every way to publicly say "my mother abuses me." Unfortunately, this rarely happens because of the child's unwillingness. Without real help, therapy, and counseling, a child can not only cope with the betrayal of his mother because he is in a subordinate role.

8.12. Tips for children

If this book ever gets to you, kids; to those of you who are suffering, contact a social work center. Tell your teacher at school, tell your neighbor, tell another family member what's going on.

You can only help yourself by seeking to spend as little time as possible at home. This way your interaction with your mother will be less. You can turn to the other parent and ask him or her for protection. It is important not to retreat into yourself, there is no way to saving yourself there. Life has already made you a "little soldier" so be brave and be a hero. Come forward and say that you are a victim of violence. If you notice this happening to someone else, tell everyone you believe can help. Tell your parents.

Don't run away from problems thinking they will magically disappear. Stand up boldly and say out loud that there is a problem. If you don't, there will never come a day when everything will stop and as you get older you will only suffer more. You will miss out on a lot of things in life and you will not even have a chance to see how beautiful life can be.

Once you know what violence is, how it manifests, who perpetrates it and how it affects the victim, go one step further and report it when you encounter it. We must not allow young lives to go out in front of our eyes just because we have made a conscious decision not to interfere. Every child deserves to have a happy life.

8.13. How can you help your child withstand the pressures of a mother with Borderline Personality Disorder?

You know best how it feels. You had to take it all yourself. That is why you are the perfect "savior" for children who need help because they live with a mother suffering from Borderline Personality Disorder. It's easier for you to recognize these kids than those who did not walk the same path.

It can be a comfort to you, knowing that you can help them. Maybe that it is one of the purposes of your life. It can help you to heal yourself and the altruism in you can greatly help these children.

You must be good and healthy first. You can only help others by first helping yourself. So don't give up and we're sure you won't. You're a fighter and that's a simple fact. You have struggled your whole life and now that you are "born again" you can speak publicly about this problem, you can advise these children, you can prevent other children from going through what you went through. In that fact lies the only beauty of what you went through. You can stop other kids from going through it. Think of all the ways you can contribute to society. You can save many and there is your power. So you have to persevere in your fight. You've already woken up and are eager to help, and tomorrow is when you can be the one to help others. It's a wonderful thought and a wonderful thing to think about. That you, from the sacrifice, may one day be a savior. That's beautiful.

CHAPTER NINE: HOW TO OVERCOME THE TRAUMA OF THE BORDERLINE MOTHER AS AN ADULT

T he cause of most psychological, emotional problems is trauma. In your cause, it was the trauma you went through due to your mother suffering from Borderline Personality Disorder. But being stuck in trauma leads to the emergence and persistence of negative symptoms such as anxiety, depression, despair, anger, helplessness, hurt, pathological possessiveness, feelings of guilt, etc. All these feelings at the level of intellect are accompanied by negative beliefs such as: "I am not worthy, Life is meaningless, I will never change, and no one will love me" and other pessimistic thoughts.

It should be emphasized that these negative emotions, as well as negative beliefs, are only symptoms of trauma, that is, indicators that trauma is still within us, that it is still activated and that it significantly affects our perception of ourselves, other people, life and the world at large. It is important not to be ashamed of your trauma because you have figuratively gone through hell. Now you have to understand what is stopping you and not letting you live life like other people. What is that little voice in our head we were talking about?

9.1. What is trauma?

Trauma is an experience of defeat, a subjective experience that involves the simultaneous experience of being threatened (emotionally or physically) and the experience that there is nothing we can do about it; that we cannot escape or avoid a situation that threatens us. Simply put, trauma is a situation in which we experience danger, and in which we judge (truly or falsely) that we do not have the resources (capacity) to protect ourselves. Trauma can be a situation that happens to us personally, but it can also occur by watching other trauma survivors. Observing people experiencing trauma can also be traumatic for the observer, especially if he or she identifies with the person experiencing the trauma.

9.2. Big and small traumas

Most people think that trauma necessarily involves experiencing some extremely bad and extremely intense experiences such as rape, war, natural disasters, etc. But many small traumas also paralyze and damage the person. Traumatic situations can be, for example, a car accident, situations involving separation from loved ones, a change of environment, all kinds of emotional, physical and sexual abuse, intimidation and harassment at work, etc.

9.3. How does trauma affect the psyche?

Trauma always occurs in a specific context, in a specific situation, and at a particular moment in time. All the traumas we have survived that we have not got rid of remain in our memory and affect us as if they were happening now and here. Whenever we find ourselves in a context reminiscent of the trauma, some of its characteristics result in the activation of trauma. When the trauma is triggered, unpleasant symptoms occur, including primarily negative emotions (anxiety, depression, anger, etc.) and bodily reactions (strain, spasm, desire to escape, numbness, etc.). At the moment when a person first experiences trauma, he or she experiences shock because, as a rule, the traumatic situation occurs unexpectedly. In a moment of shock, a person usually does not feel intense emotions, is not aware of their bodily reactions and thoughts. Symptoms of trauma begin to manifest themselves only when a person comes out of shock and that is after a certain amount of time that the person has spent safely, outside of a situation in which he or she has experienced trauma.

A good example is a soldier who has returned from the battlefield, and is now in a safe environment; he feels the symptoms of trauma (he can't stand loud sounds, has nightmares, is anxious, depressed, withdraws from people, etc.). Non-resolved trauma is reactivated over and over in all situations reminiscent of the event. What is it that reminds a person of trauma? A person is triggered by any situation that is either reminiscent of the original trauma or is a situation in which the person has the experience of being trapped. A person who has experienced trauma but has not resolved it chronically suffers from symptoms of anxiety and depression. These symptoms indicate that the trauma is still active, that it is not resolved, and that the person is making strong efforts to suppress the traumatic experience. Anxiety and depression are indicators that suppression is unsuccessful, and unsustainable in the long run. When a person can no longer tolerate anxiety or depression, he or she often takes some substances that increase the suppression of trauma and its unpleasant symptoms. A person may resort to alcohol, drugs, cigarettes, antidepressants, sedatives, etc.

9.4. Why does trauma persist and create unpleasant symptoms?

Even if the trauma took place twenty or thirty years before the present moment, how is it possible that it affects us now and here? Trauma is written in the body, that is, in memory, which triggers some bodily reactions. These bodily reactions are survival instincts. All animals (including humans) have survival instincts that are very powerful and that are triggered in situations of survival or danger. Trauma cannot exist without the activation of survival instincts. These instincts serve to keep us in a dangerous situation and allow us to survive the danger. Safety is a top priority for our bodies. The problem arises when we remain stuck in instincts that have activated. The traumatic situation has passed, we have survived, but the instincts remain activated and the body acts as if the danger is still there. Activated instincts create symptoms.

Our body expects us to release trauma, to resolve it. But we are not always able to do so. When we are unable to release trauma, it becomes trapped in the body, forcing us to suppress the painful memories. Anxiety and/or depression occur as a signal that suppression is unsustainable. Then the person tries to suppress the anxiety as well and consequently, the anxiety intensifies. Then the person may resort to drugs, alcohol or drugs.

9.5. Suppression maintains trauma and its harmful effects

As long as we suppress the trauma and its symptoms, we cannot get rid of the trauma. It affects our experience of ourselves, others and the world we live in. Secondary negative symptoms may also develop under this condition, which is usually some type of depression.

9.6. Can we permanently clear the trauma and its symptoms?

To clear the trauma, the person must first agree to it; by his own will decide that he wants to get rid of the trauma and its symptoms and take responsibility for his feelings and the changes that will occur. When a person does this, they are ready for the process.

9.7. What does the process of trauma purification look like?

The process of cleaning trauma does not involve talking about trauma or reliving the trauma. We can talk about trauma for years without any result, and the same goes for reliving emotions that are just a symptom of trauma. The process of trauma purification involves a person experiencing some of the trauma symptoms and activating the trauma through them. This does not mean that the person will relive the whole traumatic experience; it is not therapeutic and does not produce the desired results. Rather, it it is about activating the survival instincts underlying it. When instincts are activated, we can then turn them off, deactivate them. When we shut down instincts, all trauma symptoms disappear permanently, as do all accompanying bodily symptoms.

9.8. How do we know that trauma has been deactivated, purified?

When the trauma is deactivated, the person is unable to reactivate that trauma. When a person re-imagines a traumatic situation or finds himself in a similar situation, he feels nothing, is often unable to even remember the trauma; it is simply gone. When the trauma clears, all the negative symptoms that it created disappear permanently.

When we clear the key traumas, the person not only has nothing to suppress (thus no longer feeling anxiety or depression), but has access to certain conditions that were previously blocked. We call these natural state resources. These resources are love, self-love, freedom, a sense of our boundaries, security, etc.

Each person walks through life collecting different experiences. Life is about gathering experiences and applying them and exploiting them in future situations. That's a real skill. We all love it when it we experience positive and happy experiences, those that bring us peace, satisfaction, pleasure, joy and put a smile on our face. We enjoy them and want to be constantly in the state that happy experiences bring us. But what happens when we experience a distressing, negative experience that we feel has characterized us and causes negative emotions that we cannot possibly get rid of? Most people like you are trapped in traumas of the past, dating back to childhood. You've survived much, much more than a soldier in the war, but now it's time to let go of the trauma. We have said many times that you have to let go of your memories – that little voice in your head has to go away. The biggest problem is the transfer of memories and a return to the past.

9.9. Transferring memories

Emotional memories are stored in our cells. When they are negative, they often remain unclear. This usually causes many physical and mental illnesses to develop. Our cells are always being renewed. Different cells are renewed at different speeds. Liver cells take 6 weeks to recover, while skin cells take 3 to 4 weeks. Our eye cells are completely renewed every two days.

9.10. The cells are complete

However, old memories remain in our cells. These old memories can cause decaying diseased patterns within the cells. And before the old station dies, it transfers its memory to the next station.

94

9.11. How to break that vicious circle?

The memory must be detected first. Some people know which trauma is keeping them captive, while some are unaware of it, that is, they have forgotten or suppressed it. But they feel the impact on their health, despite being unable to remember. But that's where your biggest asset lies; you know your trauma: your childhood and your mother with Borderline Personality Disorder.

9.12. How to overcome traumatic events

The general concept that trauma can still bring about positive change is a common theme that emerged in religious and philosophical teachings thousands of years ago, but it wasn't until the mid-1990s that the term "post-traumatic growth" was coined by psychologists Richard Tedeschi and Lawrence Calhoun. Tedeschi and Calhoun argue that post-trauma growth and recovery occur in five general areas:

- Respect for life

- Relationship with others

- New opportunities in life

- Personal strength

- Spiritual change

In addition to these five factors, there are many other items developed by these psychologists to determine an individual's progress in the area of the personal, observing others, and the meaning of events while dealing with the consequences of trauma. This approach involves dealing with post-traumatic stress, but also offers a new lens through which an individual can explore himself in the shadow of trauma.

This approach entails, first and foremost, empathy for patients and an understanding of their condition, rather than alleviating their suffering and moving on to proposing practical solutions. Most often, the help of a psychologist/psychiatrist/psychotherapist is sought after a traumatic event has occurred. Psychotherapy can help you see that things like this are true and possible:

- I found that I was stronger than I thought.

- Now I know I can handle it better.

- I have changed priorities about what is important in life.

Learning and growing from our own experience allows healing to take place in "real-time" – we are not just talking about it, we are getting into it.

Here's an example we believe you will see yourself in. A patient called Tanya (35) suffered psychiatric abuse from the age of 8 to 13. Tanya constantly felt lonely and distrustful of others and started the process of psychotherapy. In several psychodrama group therapies, Tanya experienced the support of group members by having people in the group stand behind her, hands on her shoulders in support, as she talked about her traumas. She received hugs when she cried or felt scared. Group members contacted her between sessions to see how she was feeling and progressing. At the end of the three-month therapy, Tanya said, "Because the members of my group were there for me, and they supported me when I was crying and when I was in pain, I was more likely to be able to count on others during difficult times."

9.13. What other methods can help overcome traumatic events?

Post-traumatic Stress Disorder is not a terminal illness. It can be treated with experiential methods such as group therapy for psycho-drama, which deals with trauma in progress. As clients collectively build the strength to cope with their trauma, they realize that they can become winners in dealing with it.

Psychotherapists also recommend that story writing be used as an experiential strategy for identifying, clarifying, and solidifying post-traumatic recovery. Because every time we describe the events of our lives, we provide and discover the basic patterns of their meaning. It is the meaning of our experience that shapes how we feel, think and re-act.

No matter how difficult things were and the events you went through, it is important for you to understand that post-traumatic recovery and growth is a normal process that may be an opportunity for you to build a new life.

"These are wounds that never appear on the body, but that are deeper and more painful than anything that bleeds," wrote Lorel K. Hamilton. When we are physically wounded, the world sympathizes with us. We get sick leave, social assistance, and medical care. Unfortunately, when our emotions are hurt, most of this is missing. We have to create it ourselves.

Emotional trauma forces you to be your own hero. Here are six tips to help you do just that and let go of a bad childhood, your mother and that little voice in your head.

1. Give Priority to Taking Care of Yourself

For many of us, it is natural that we care most about our loved ones. We often do this at the expense of fulfilling our own lives. Unfortunately, you cannot pour from an empty glass. Caring for yourself must come first, especially for those who care for others. Look at yourself honestly, carefully and with love. Determine your needs. Do you need time in silence every day? Counseling or group therapy? Useful service work? An artistic expression? Relaxation? A weekend trip to reconnect with your spirit? Give these needs priority. Fill them without remorse.

2. Become Grateful

When we struggle with emotional demons, it can become natural for us to focus on the darkness in our lives. Instead, turn your eyes to the light. As often as you can, take a break to identify the five things that you are grateful for. They do not have to be deep or significant. Just be good enough. For example, I am currently grateful for water, sun, music, bed, and the internet. This exercise is simple but very effective. It changes our worldview. The world around us starts to look brighter, happier and more forgiving. By acting in the world with gratitude, we can transform it into the place we want it to be.

3. Respect Your Body

When emotions are challenged, it is normal for us to allow our physical health to deteriorate. Unfortunately, this is the opposite of what we need. When our body is healthy, our mind is clearer. Emotions come under our control. Our spirit is capable of dealing with the world better. Make sure you sleep enough. Stay hydrated. Exercise in a way that suits you, moderately or rigorously, indoors or out, alone or in a group. Eat the foods that supply your body with the nutrients it deserves. Stay away from the scales. This is not about how you look or how your clothes look. What matters here is how you feel.

4. Build a Support Network

The worst part of any trauma is the feeling of being alone in it. As human beings, we are not created to face challenges ourselves. We need emotional support. Because of this, there is a support group for almost every major emotional challenge. From depression to addiction, incurable illness to sexual assault, there is certainly a group with people like you. First, you enjoy the warm relief that you are no longer alone in your fight. Then, allow them to share their experience, strength, and hope.

5. Communicate Honestly

Bad will and intolerance grows in you as long as you keep them. If you have a problem with a loved one, let them know. Tell her how she hurt you. Put your feelings on the table, calmly and kindly. This is how you give yourself the freedom to forgive. Remember, forgiveness is not about the other person. It's about your decision to let go of the hurt and get on with life. Don't let the other person's unkindness have power over your heart for a day.

6. Write your story

When our hardest feelings remain in us, they become stronger. There is something liberating in the decision to put them on paper instead. Use the pen to regain power. Let the words flow, and then read them to yourself. This is how you allow your mind to create new insight and perspective. You also allow your emotions to be released from your brain and body and find a new home on paper.

"Anything human can be mentioned, and anything that can be mentioned is manageable. When we talk about our feelings, they become less burdensome, less poignant, and less scary. The people we confide in with this important conversation can help us know that we are not alone," Fred Rogers wrote. If you are injured, do not hide. Fight. Connect with others and connect with yourself. Love yourself enough to heal your wounds.

Your trauma is great without a doubt. But you have done a lot of things for yourself just by reading this book. Now you have to persevere. The most important thing is that now, more than ever you believe in yourself, we believe in you because you have almost come to the end of the book. You are aware of yourself and the confusion that has occurred. Now is the time to "feed the good wolf," to rise above what was and to leave the past where it belongs.

My grandmother once told me something that I still carry with me and that takes me through life and now I will share it with you. She said to me "Son, you are a blacksmith of your fortune."

CHAPTER TEN: START YOUR HEALING PROCESS

You've come to the last chapter of this book. Congratulations on your persistence and for the fact that you have started your healing process. This has been a long journey.

You would never have read this book if you did not want deep answers. You wanted to find out if there was a way to live better, to be a better person. Not to be the one hiding behind the mask because he is afraid to show himself and have a normal interaction with others.

All your life you've stood by and watched other people happy and content with their lives. You tried to get away from others, you had no one to turn to because you didn't trust anyone. The sad truth is that this is a very sensitive topic without many people being aware of how painful and severe it is. Borderline Personality Disorder is a condition that is difficult in itself, and when the mother is the abuser and the child is a victim, as in this story, it becomes an even more difficult topic.

Now that you know everything, your path to healing can begin. But there are a few things you need to do to finally move forward and start a new happy part of your life story.

10.1. Forgive your mother

To forgive means to get rid of the hurt and the need to punish the one who hurt us. Don't hold on to the past and resent your mother. We kept saying – she never consciously wanted you to be hurt. To forgive involves letting go of anger and feelings of shame, as well as getting rid of the need to talk again about a painful event and how to hurt we are. Forgiveness has nothing to do with the person who hurt you, forgiveness is what will bring you relief and deliverance and what allows you to continue on your path to what you want.

To forgive does not mean to forget, because it is impossible, and the mere memory of the event serves us not to make the same or similar mistakes in the future.

10.2. Spiritual prerequisites

First of all, it must be understood that at the spiritual level, each injury has long been agreed upon. We agreed with the people who would hurt us long ago, before coming to this planet, what they would do to us and what we would learn through that lesson. Of course, there is spiritual amnesia and we are not aware of it throughout our lives, but that does not mean that there is no prerequisite.

In my experience, the people who hurt us are our most important teachers and the people who have enabled us to grow the most. A lot of people in this form get their "wake up call" and thus begin their spiritual growth.

10.3. Forgiveness is a process that takes time

It is one thing to make a mental decision to forgive, and it is quite another to truly forgive, to get rid of toxic feelings and replace them with compassion. Spiritual bypass happens when, knowing that it is good to forgive, we neglect to be deeply hurt on an emotional level. We must process and release all emotions associated with the event. That is why it is important to face our feelings we feel and release them. Forgiveness takes time; it is a process.

10.4. Giving up judgment

To truly forgive someone, we need to completely give up condemnation, what we believe to be just, unjust, bad and good, and look at the whole story from a higher perspective. Understand that it happened to us because our soul has chosen such a lesson. Not only did we choose, but we also needed to grow, so it was important to learn. Forgiveness is one of the most powerful things we can do for ourselves and it brings about a great transformation when it happens.

10.5. Pitfalls in the process of forgiveness

The whole process of forgiveness is hampered by what is called the "victim concept" that can be found in almost every one of us. It is necessary to recognize this part of yourself and to change it gently. Our ego loves to be right and that is why we remain stuck in our anger and feel injustice for longer. The trap we often fall into is that we think we would never do something like that. Getting rid of expectations from others but also from ourselves is perhaps the most beautiful gift we can give ourselves because all disappointments come from it. If we drop expectations then there will be no disappointment.

10.6. To forgive means to give yourself love

Forgiving someone means actively applying love for oneself. And as you have probably experienced, the most difficult person to forgive is yourself. So give special attention to this process and get yourself out of the door, stop expecting perfection from yourself, give yourself permission to make a mistake and just be more laid back with yourself and others.

10.7. At every moment, each of us does the best we can

The truth is that the person who hurt us is a being who has also been deeply hurt and who did not know how to do better than she did. This is a person who has not healed their wounds. It is the same with us; until we heal our wounds, we hurt ourselves and others. Essentially, each of us does the best we can in the circumstances.

10.8. Let go of the past

Do you regularly lose yourself in sad and bitter thoughts about past events in your life? Do you often find it futile to try because everything will "turn out bad again?"

We humans are always on the lookout for patterns in our experience. In this way, we make sense of everything that happens to us and the world around us. This system works pretty well for most things and has been the driver of our evolution. It helps us to decide more easily what action i.e. action to take when confronted with a new situation and experience.

10.9. Why is it so difficult sometimes to let go of the past, even when we try?

In some cases, we may have problems with the disagreement between the facts as if it were some "system error" that appears in our mental software. This usually happens when it comes to strong emotions. Most likely, we will remember very clearly and vividly the things we have strong feelings about. These patterns will, therefore, make our choices stronger than others.

So, if some disturbing or sad events or situations from our past are also very emotional for us, they can grow quite big in our heads, making us hyper-sensitive to similar patterns in the present. We make a connection between things of the past and things that seem similar to us in the present, even when they are not very similar. It's like "cleaning everything with the same cloth."

For example, someone who was previously in a very unhappy relationship may find themselves in a situation of fear and anger, even when the present relationship is good. They create the wrong link between the old and the new situation based on the learned pattern of connections from the past that can cause unexpected difficulties in the current relationship.

To let go of the past, you need to change how you feel about those events. Of course, we cannot undo what happened in our past. So, are we doomed to live with such "broken links" and their unintended consequences forever? Are we stuck surviving what happened over and over, wishing it was different? Of course not, because even though history cannot be restarted, we can change how we feel about it. And we can do this by eliminating the emotional toll on past events, emotionally distancing ourselves from them all. This involves making an emotional change within us and finding a healthier, more positive view of those events of the past.

When you start living day by day and when you learn to fully indulge, you will experience a range of benefits. Nobody likes bad times because they harm our mood and mind. All of us have a past filled with bad memories and days that we may regret, but it's never good to think about the past. When you learn to live in the present and let go of the past, positivity and hope will come into your life.

10.10. Avoid bad moods

We all have bad days and times when we are not in the best of moods. Living in the past can cause a bad mood, and this attracts and spreads negative energy. That's how you create a negative and unhealthy environment, and no one wants to live that way.

10.11. Start living a new life

Have you ever caught yourself living in the past, thinking about bad memories, situations, and problems? This happens occasionally to everyone, especially when we are doing something that reminds us of the past. It can be frustrating! That is why it is important to combat this mindset. You need to forget the past and continue living. Life always goes on.

10.12. Relieve stress

Stress is the worst and strongest enemy. With a hectic lifestyle, stress can rarely be completely resolved. Still, that doesn't mean you don't have to try and try to eliminate stress. One way is to stop living in the past. Doing so will remove one of the leading sources of stress; focus on the future, and stop worrying about the past.

10.13. You can't change anything

One important question that will help you stop thinking so much about the past is: can you go back in time and change certain events? The answer is, definitely not. No matter how dissatisfied you are with your past, always remember that you can do absolutely nothing about it.

10.14. Learn how to take control and become happy

Another reason you need to stop thinking about the past and start living in the present is positivity. Positivity is an important part of life that helps make peace, adopt healthy habits, and bring positivity to life.

10.15. Release your fear

Fears are usually very difficult to deal with, and one of the reasons for their appearance is the lack of courage to deal with them. One way to stop living in fear is to indulge yourself and stop thinking about the past and certain events that caused you to live in fear.

10.16. What steals your inner peace?

Are you addicted to something? If you are currently experiencing addiction, try to stop it because it will make your life better. If you stop being addicted to something, then keep that attitude. Make sure you completely forget that you have ever been addicted to anything.

10.17. Love yourself

If you think about the past and some of the bad events that you have faced and what you resent about yourself, you will certainly not be happy. Live in the present and stop thinking about the past because it will bring you love for yourself.

10.18. Get happier

The health of the body is very important when it comes to being able to live a fulfilled life. Poor health will make it difficult to perform certain activities, and you certainly do not want to be that kind of person. Get rid of the past and focus on the present, because then you will become healthier and, ultimately, happier.

10.19. Make new friends

Friends are a necessary part of life; without them life would not make sense. Good friends make our days happier and more beautiful. If you live in the past, all you have to think about is problems and you will continue to believe that no one wants you. You need to think solely about the present because it will give you confidence and will attract new people into your life.

10.20. Yesterday is history

What has happened in the past is now unattainable. Given that the past cannot be changed, the future is the only point in focus.

10.21. The present is important

The past is important and it is something we can learn from. In the present, where you live and act, you need to stop worrying about the past and become interested solely in the present.

Freedom is a blessing that cannot be replaced by anything else. Freedom is about doing whatever you want whenever you want. Don't limit yourself and stop being a slave to the past. Always think only about the present and how you can learn from past mistakes.

10.22. The past affects your present abilities

Have you ever thought that the past can cause your present abilities to decline? The past can have such an impact on your abilities that you will start to feel like you have made a lot of mistakes and are still making them. This is why you need to forget the past to eliminate these thoughts.

10.23. Become successful

Who among us does not want to be successful, feel independent and do the things we have only dreamed of? Success doesn't just happen; you need to act, be patient and move forward. One way to achieve this is to leave the past behind and start living in the present.

10.24. Make your days happy

Happiness is something that needs to be strived for every day. Happiness is contagious and brings benefits not only to you but to the people around you. This way you build a healthy and positive living environment.

10.25. Avoid creating problems

Who wants extra problems? Do not create problems where there are none. It will affect you physically, morally and emotionally. If you continue to live in the past and stop hoping for a beautiful and bright future, you will create additional and unnecessary problems.

10.26. Stop being depressed

Depression is characterized by intense sadness caused by various events. Depression can cause many problems. You should do your best to avoid it and practice positive thinking and optimism. One of the leading causes of depression is thinking about the past.

10.27. Work on confidence

Self-confidence is the way we experience our abilities. Focusing on the past will never boost your confidence. Living in the moment while ignoring the past can help boost your confidence.

10.28. Set a goal

Setting goals is what will encourage you to achieve your dreams. Thinking about the past will discourage you from setting goals because you will think that you will never succeed.

10.29. Be a role model

It will have a positive effect on your life and be a pleasure for you. When you think about being someone's role model, you will instinctively start living the best you can, because only then will you be able to advise others to do the same.

10.30. Be positive

Positive thinking is a state of mind in which thoughts, images, and ideas with positive effects inhabit, grow and spread, cheering a man on and filling his glass forever so that it is not half empty. Negative thoughts are said to attract negative situations, and positive ones are good, joyful and blessed. Therefore, changing your attitude for the better will help you to create your life exactly the way you want it.

The power of positive thinking should be gradually built up and only then will you help reap its fruits.

If you decide to build your life on an ever-optimistic basis, read below about the benefits of positive thinking.

10.31. More energy

Sometimes fatigue is in the brain and mind, not in the body. If you are positive you will forever fly on the wings of good energy. You will find it easier to cope with day-to-day situations and to cross any obstacles that come your way.

10.32. Better health

The way of thinking greatly affects the functions of the body. When you replace negative thoughts with calmness and self-confidence, the anxiety and worry will just disappear. It also means that the muscles in your body will relax and any disturbance of sleep and fatigue will be absent. Positive people also suffer less from depression. So start being positive – now.

10.33. Start creating a new chapter in life

So far, your life has not even come close to being good. There is no doubt about that. You never received anything; you were not appreciated enough, as a child you suffered a lot. It's time to close that chapter in your life.

Teach yourself to live your life to the fullest. Turn your head to the other side. There is no need to wear a mask, no need to hide. Forgive your mother, let go of the past, and be positive.

Seek the help of an expert to guide you towards healing, but most importantly, have the will. Will is the key, will has led you to this book and you have already made the first steps.

This book ends, but your story is just beginning. You are closing the cover, but at the same time, you are opening the cover of a new, happy and beautiful story. And remember - you are the blacksmith of your fortune.

CONCLUSION

In this book, we have touched on a very sensitive topic. We talked about Borderline Personality Disorder and how this condition can affect life. It is important to know how dangerous Borderline Personality Disorder is, and hopefully we have been able to reach people. People need to become familiar with this topic. People need to learn about this topic because it has not been sufficiently studied. This book is even more important because it emphasizes a critical point in this condition. In this book, we have touched on the relationship between a mother suffering from Borderline Personality Disorder and a child who is in a victim position.

This book defines this condition and serves as a guide to identifying Borderline Personality Disorder, and through the chapters you will have found out everything you need to recognize the condition, to spot symptoms that can often be so masked that they are almost impossible to recognize. This book is will help you see these symptoms and respond appropriately. This is a serious problem and it is even more significant when you bear in mind that victims are the most sensitive social category – children. Through the book, you have learned what Borderline Personality Disorder is, what the different types of Borderline Personality Disorder are, and how a mother suffering from this condition behaves. We have also examined how it affects the child, how can the child be protected, what the main problems these children face are, how children may feel like victims and what the consequences of this toxic mother-child relationship are.

The most important part of this book is the healing process. We believe that if you have gone through everything in the book, you can protect yourself, act preventively, and keep yourself safe. You must know that you are not alone and that you can look at life with fresh eyes. You were a victim, but that doesn't mean you can't get your life back.

You need to understand that life has no reprise. You only have one life and you should not live as a victim. Help yourself and know that you will succeed. All you need is to be persistent, to let go of the past, and to move boldly forward.

Because of this, love yourself and know that you are the only driver in your life.